SCM STUDYGUIDE TO THE SACRAMENTS

SCM STUDYGUIDE TO THE SACRAMENTS

Ross Thompson

scm press

Scripture quotations are from the New Revised Standard Version of
the Bible, copyright 1989 by the Division of Christian Education of
the National Council of the Churches of Christ in the USA. Used by
permission. All rights reserved.

British Library Cataloguing in Publication data

A catalogue record for this book is available
from the British Library

0 334 04020 5/978 0 334 04020 0

First published in 2006 by SCM Press
9–17 St Albans Place, London N1 0NX

www.scm-canterburypress.co.uk

SCM Press is a division of
SCM-Canterbury Press Ltd

Typeset by Regent Typesetting, London
Printed and bound in Great Britain by
Creative Print and Design, Wales

Contents

Preface

This book has arisen from the convergence of several processes, some long-term, some short, for which in the spirit of the book, 'it is right to give thanks and praise'.

In the longest term the book emerges from a lifelong interest in signs and symbols, including the reading and writing of poetry. I have long believed in a 'sacramental' universe, and that the seamless unity of meaning and matter we find in the sacraments springs from Christ and cosmos, in a manner explored in my *Holy Ground, the Spirituality of Matter*. I give thanks for Dr Denys Turner (now professor) for directing these explorations in my doctoral thesis,[1] and for leading me to authors that have been important in the writing of this book, not least Fr Herbert McCabe.

Again long term, this book could not have been written had I not been nourished by the sacraments myself, and experienced as parish priest the life they brought to others. So I thank the congregations I have served, and also thank the Orthodox Church for the liturgy that has been specially formative for my own understanding, and especially the writings of Fr Alexander Schmemann.

More immediately, the book has developed out of a module I taught at Cardiff University and St Michael's College, Llandaff. Joseph Martos' *Doors to the Sacred* was the key textbook for that module, so it has been seminal for this book. The interaction with and feedback from intelligent students has been a joy to me and this book could not have been written without it.

Finally, I thank Barbara Laing of SCM Press for inviting me to write the book, and my wife, Judith, for the support she has given and the patience with which she has accepted the hours I have spent communing with nothing but a computer screen!

Further Reading

Ross Thompson, 1991, *Holy Ground, the Spirituality of Matter*, London: SPCK.
Joseph Martos, 2001, *Doors to the Sacred: A historical introduction to the sacraments in the Catholic Church*, Liguori, Missouri: Liguori/Triumph.

Introduction

Here is something about the methodology and theological approach taken in this book, something about what it aims to achieve and ways in which it can be used, and an explanation of its structure.

Method and Approach

There are at least three ways of knowing a human phenomenon like the sacraments:

1   We can ask what kind of phenomenon it is, asking questions like, what causes people to do it, or what function does the phenomenon have in society. Here we will be looking to explain things by general theories in the human sciences, such as history and sociology. This gives an 'outsider' description; the less the describer is involved in and committed to the values of the participants, the more she is able to give such a description, amounting to an *explanation* of the phenomenon.

2   Alternatively, we can ask how the participants themselves understand what they are doing, what account do they give of it, what does it mean to them. Here empathy may become more important than science, and reasons more relevant than causes. We are looking for an 'insider' description. The more we can involve ourselves with the participants and commit ourselves to, or at least suspend disbelief about, their values, the better our *understanding* of the phenomenon.

3 But a third possibility is to ask what the things say about the people. We can investigate the phenomena themselves, and ask whether they suggest new ways of understanding the context in which they are set. Here the phenomenon supplies an explanation of itself; general understanding is subjugated to the particular. We are looking to the phenomenon for *disclosure*.

Take as an example the life story of Winston Churchill:

1 Explanation will place him in his context, looking at his upbringing and the political scene and social setting of his life, trying to understand how these factors made him act as he did.

2 Reading his autobiography, letters and other documents will show his own understanding of his actions.

3 Asking what Churchill's actions say about him and his time, looking especially for acts which somehow disclose his personality or the meaning of his times in a new way.

Explanation, understanding and disclosure each contribute to our knowledge of a human phenomenon, and a full comprehension involves an interaction between all three modes. This is our endeavour in the case of the sacraments, and explains the structure of the book.

Although throughout we will be looking for interaction of all three modes, in Chapter 1 we will seek an outsider's view, and ask what kind of human phenomenon the sacraments are. We will be looking at the sociology and the history of the sacraments.

However, as we move through the rest of Part 1 and on into Part 2 we will be balancing this approach with a consideration of how the different denominations have understood their sacraments. Here we will be looking at theologies of the sacraments, of the kind that we find in many traditional authors like Thomas Aquinas, and in more recent ones, like Kenan Osbourne (1988).

Finally, when we turn to consider the different sacraments in detail, in Parts 3, 4 and 5, we will mix in the third approach. We will ask whether there is a theology, a sociology, a history, or a politics implicit in the sacraments themselves. So we will do a little sacramental theology, of the kind developed by the Russian Orthodox Alexander Schmemann (2002), and the

Roman Catholic Aidan Kavanagh (1981), authors who try to step aside from what they call 'secondary theology' – the theology of creeds and systematics – to derive a 'primary theology' from the liturgy itself. Here we are not using sociology or theology to understand the liturgy, but using the liturgy to understand society and theology.

All this involves seeking a precarious balance between what are fundamentally different theological methods that generally present themselves as opposed:

- *Liberal theology* has traditionally looked first to an understanding of what is general to humanity – understanding gleaned through history, sociology or psychology – and fitted theological accounts to this general basis.
- *Traditional theology* has looked rather to the church's own self-understanding, through its own pronouncements about itself and God, seeing these as definitive for our understanding of humanity.
- *Neo-orthodox theology*, based on the work of Karl Barth and more recently the 'radical orthodox' theology of John Milbank and others, has taken the third line, regarding the phenomenon of Jesus Christ, or the liturgy itself (Pickstock, 1998) as disclosing the ultimate, and demanding a total reappraisal of human history and society in its own terms.

The approach in this book will be less straightforward than any of these. Here we shall be letting the sacraments speak for themselves and interpret for us the human and the divine. The approach we take here is not blind to the fact that the sacraments are humanly evolved phenomena needing to be approached both through the human sciences and through the understandings of participants. Where simpler approaches reduce the understanding of the sacraments to a monologue, in which only sociology, or only the church, or only the sacraments themselves, are allowed to pronounce about themselves and the others, this approach will allow a three-way dialogue to proceed as a kind of polyphony in three voices, in which each interprets and is interpreted by the others.

Aims and Use

This Studyguide has three main aims:

First, it presents the developing views of the sacraments in the different denominations with as much vividness, clarity and ecumenical impartiality as possible. The book is for a core audience of Level 1 university students, where it would adapt easily to the teaching of a 20-credit module, or used selectively, a smaller module. But this means the book should be approachable for a wide variety of equivalent readers as it guides the reader through difficult, but surprisingly rewarding, concepts. Not least of the rewards is the fact that, contrary to received opinion, it is not simple faith but theological rigour that is the friend of ecumenism. It is when we wrestle with concepts we realize there are different ways of thinking the same thing, and ideas that have been barriers can come tumbling down.

Second, the book invites readers to explore these views for themselves. This is an introduction, and the aim is to stimulate reading of primary texts, not to substitute for it. So pointers are supplied to help students put various theologians on the map, as it were, rather than trying to give a complete account of their thinking. On the other hand, a number of fairly deep and difficult thinkers, are introduced in the belief that ideas, if valid, can always be presented in relatively simple terms, and ideas that can only be obscure are likely to be obscurantist.

This aim has informed the presentation of different ways of looking at the sacraments, and the repeated invitations to discuss or ponder specific questions. The book leaves lots of questions deliberately unresolved. It is up to the reader to decide upon answers by examining the sketches of different possible approaches and pondering the questions, until the reader's own answers begin to form.

Finally, however, it has to be admitted that the author is no more impartial than anyone on the sacraments. My own stance, as an Anglican with Eastern Orthodox yearnings and a strong nonconformist streak, is in a sense ecumenical in itself. But it has to be said that I am passionate about the sacraments as a way of shaping a rich vision and a broad way of Christian life. So I would like to see the sacraments becoming central to the formation of future ministers of word and sacrament in all denominations, because I would like to see ministers who are passionate and understanding regarding the chief things they are there to administer. I would also invite those who are simply exploring Christianity out of interest to see the sacraments, not as esoteric specialities for the faithful, but as a good place to begin exploring Christian life and theology as a whole.

Structure

This is fairly self-explanatory. The book divides into five parts. Part 1 explores origins, investigating in successive chapters the general human need for rite, Hebrew developments, and Jesus and the New Testament. Part 2 looks at sacraments in general, moving from the historical consideration of how Christians have understood them, in the first chapter, to a consideration of themes, issues and possibilities today. Then Parts 3 and 4 look at the sacraments of initiation (mainly baptism), and the eucharist respectively. The focus is on these because they are the ecumenically accepted sacraments, because they are the sacraments all Christians will have experienced, because an in-depth treatment of two or three sacraments seemed to promise more by way of an understanding of sacraments generally than an equal but superficial treatment of them all, and because these sacraments are key to any understanding of the church and promise most in terms of broad theological vision. In both Parts there is a move from a historical treatment in the first chapter to a development of themes, issues and opportunities in the other(s). Finally, in Part 5, the understanding we have gleaned in earlier chapters will help us to understand the remaining five rites that the Catholic Church considers sacraments. Though the exploration here will be a relatively swift overview, it is undertaken from a vantage point that will impart some depth.

Finally, it is worth noting that some good material supplementary to this guide is available both on my own website www.holydust.org, and the companion site to this book, hosted on the SCM Press website. Go to www.scmpress.co.uk/studyguidesacraments. Unlike the Studyguide, these sites will be updated with new developments, and will contain forums where readers can pool their own questions, feedback and ideas. I invite the reader to have a regular browse on both, and so belong to an ongoing community gathered round the Studyguide.

Bible quotations are from the New Revised Standard Version.

Further Reading

All are relevant to the book as a whole.

D. M. Baillie, 1964, *The Theology of the Sacraments*, London: Faber.

P. Béguerie and C. Duchesneau, 1980, *How to Understand the Sacraments*, London: SCM Press.

Peter Fink (ed.), 1991, *New Dictionary of Sacramental Worship*, Collegeville, Minnesota: The Liturgical Press.

Tad Guzie, 1981, *The Book of Sacramental Basics*, Mahwah and New York: Paulist Press.

Aidan Kavanagh, 1981, *On Liturgical Theology*, Collegeville, Minnesota: The Liturgical Press.

John Macquarrie, 1997, *A Guide to the Sacraments*, London: SCM Press.

Joseph Martos, 2001, *Doors to the Sacred: A historical introduction to the sacraments of the Catholic Church* (revised edition), Ligouri, Missouri: Ligouri/Triumph.

Herbert McCabe, 1964, *The New Creation*, London and Melbourne: Sheed and Ward.

Kenan Osbourbne OFM, 1988, *Sacramental Theology: A General Introduction*, Mahwah and New York: Paulist Press.

Catherine Pickstock, 1998, *After Writing: On the liturgical consummation of philosophy*, Oxford and Massachusetts: Oxford University Press. An obscure but courageous work which looks to the old Latin mass for an entire interpretation of reality.

Alexander Schmemann, 2002, *For the Life of the World: Sacraments and Orthodoxy*, New York: St Vladimir's Seminary Press (originally published in 1966 by Darton, Longman and Todd as *The World as Sacrament*).

Part 1

Meanings and Origins

1

Symbol and Rite in Three Dimensions

In the light of the method sketched in the Introduction, we begin by asking what kind of general human phenomenon a sacrament is, trying to see the sacraments with the eyes of a total outsider.

Few would deny that sacraments are rites. Some might deny they are rituals, but this is perhaps more because the latter term has acquired in the modern consciousness a negative connotation (see later) beyond its basic meaning, which clearly relates to the term 'rite'. To avoid these negative connotations I shall generally prefer the term 'rite', but where I use 'ritual' I intend this in the original and more recent sociological sense which makes no value judgement.

So what might rites – including sacraments – be and do for human beings?

Sacraments for Martians

We can begin this by imagining a group of observers who have excellent intelligence and are good at producing theories that explain things, but have no instinctive empathy with humans, and no ability to share in people's understanding of what they do. They will have the same basic instincts as humans so as to be able to understand the motivations of sex and self-preservation which explain what we do at the basic level, and they will have great ability to build on this basis to advance theories to *explain* conduct. But they will not share any human language or culture, and will not empathize with humans, so they will not be able to *understand* our own explanations. Nor – perhaps obviously – will the sacraments or any other human phenomenon *disclose* their own meaning to such observers. We can imagine these observers as rational beings from another planet, say Mars.

Exercise (maybe in groups for each numbered item)

What would such Martians understand and fail to understand about each of the following? What in each phenomenon (if anything) would you describe as having a dimension of rite?
1 Amazonians hunting in the rain-forest.
2 A fox-hunt in rural England.
3 People going to work on the tube.
4 A meal at McDonalds.
5 The lighting of candles at a birthday celebration.
6 A eucharist.
7 A football match.
8 Bathing a baby.
9 A baptism.

In the first case the Martians would clearly understand the Amazonians' hunt for food, though there may be other aspects – maybe special dress, or dances before or after the hunt – that would not be so easily explained. These we might call rites. The Martians might try to interpret the fox-hunt on similar lines. However, the disproportionate amount of effort, colour and pageantry attached to the catching of this meagre food item, which is not eaten anyway, would show that in a fox-hunt we are dealing with a kind of rite. (That of course is why people defend fox-hunting with religious zeal; were it just a pragmatic question of the best way to control the fox population, nobody would be so bothered.)

The same considerations apply elsewhere. The Martians would probably be able to work out the relation between going to work and having food and a nice environment to live in. They may work out that the footballers are earning a living. But why so many gather to watch this repetitive series of kicks to a small round object, and to respond with repeated chants and wavings of banners and rattles, would probably remain a *mystery* to them (a concept to which we shall return). Remember, the Martians do not have concepts like 'worship' to interpret such repeated activity!

Again, our Martians would probably understand fast food, whether or not they had their own Martian equivalent of McDonalds! But why light candles at some meals, and why so little food at a eucharist? And they might recognize the hygienic reasons for washing babies. But why go through the motions of washing at a baptism where there is only enough water to cleanse a little bit of the baby's head?

We can venture this hypothesis: we describe actions as rites when a) they are often repeated in the same or similar pattern and b) they are a mystery to Martians. In other words a rite is a repeated action that derives its meaning from its human context of ideas, rather than from practical needs. Rites are repeated human actions that serve to enact or express human ideas. So we cannot explain rites except by understanding them.

Sacraments as Christian Rites

As well as involving repeated actions, rites generally but not always involve special people to do them – priests or ministers – special places to do them in – temples, mosques, churches – and special times to undertake them – in the week, the year, the lunar cycle or occasions in life. All these special requirements have often been applied to the way sacraments have been celebrated, though only the first has generally been regarded as essential to make something a sacrament.

Sacraments are Christian rites in the sense that they are repeated Christian actions that serve to enact or express Christian ideas. Originally, as we shall see, the term was used to describe all such Christian actions – the saying of the Lord's prayer and creed, the reading of the scriptures in worship, processions with lit candles, and the like, were all 'sacraments'. Later the term was narrowed down to just seven, or just two, such actions. So now in most churches, the sacraments are all rites, though not all rites are sacraments.

In addition, in the eighteenth-century Enlightenment many people came to believe that everything should be regulated by reason, not religion or divine command. 'Rite', and especially the connected term 'ritual' came to acquire negative connotations of something irrational, primitive, dark, obscure and perhaps sinister. So we commonly use 'rite', 'ritual' and 'ritualistic' in a negative way, to denote an action performed obsessively for no clear reason, like avoiding stepping on cracks in the pavement. Here the rite is performed not to express a shared human meaning but because of some inner personal meaning or compulsion. Psychologists such as Sigmund Freud have made us aware of this dark, obsessive side of religion and rite, and the irrational, possessive, demanding idea of God it often seeks to placate. But such obsessive 'works' are inappropriate from a Christian point of view since, as Luther argued, they imply a basic lack of faith in God, and a misguided attempt to win God's love as if it were not already there.

Positive and Negative Rite

All religions involve rite, because all are attempting to express a transcendent meaning through human actions and human society. In some religions there is a lot of 'positive rite'. But arguably we may speak also of 'negative rite', where something is forbidden. Thus Jews and Muslims not eating pork can be seen as a negative rite. Catholic and Orthodox worship can be seen as full of positive rite (incense, icons, genuflections, bowings, processions, etc.) while Protestant worship has more negative rite (not using such things, sabbath observance). And people can be as obsessive and 'ritualistic' about the things they do not do as others are about what they feel is the right way to do things. There is a sacramental quality, some argue, about the austerity of Quaker worship: complete lack of hymns, readings, symbols and rites, just silence in a bare room.

On this understanding, non-ritualistic worship would be worship where what is done is neither rigidly prescribed nor proscribed, but varies according to what the people desire or feel appropriate to the occasion, on aesthetic, practical, spiritual or other grounds, following perhaps the advice of St Paul, 'all things are lawful, but not all are beneficial' (1 Cor. 6.12).

> ### Discussion
>
> Is this understanding of positive and negative rite helpful?
> What positive and negative rites do you find in churches you are
> familiar with, and what things are decided on a non-ritualistic
> basis?

Six Ways to Understand Rites

So to our central question: What gives meaning to rites? Anthropologists
and sociologists have proposed a number of factors. The following six headings try to cover the broad range of proposals that have been made, without
being definitive.[1]

1 **Myth** Typically religions tell stories in which the holy is transposed into
   a sacred time: a creation or golden age in the past, or the life story of an
   ideal historical figure like Buddha or Christ. The rite may retell this story
   in such a way that people's own story is taken up into and related to the
   sacred time. Often the rite involves the obedience to the past we call tradition. Typically, the story may describe how the gods themselves have
   instituted the rite and commanded humans to continue them.
2 **Magic or future effect** As well as relating to the past, ritual is used to cause
   a definite effect in the future. Often the desired effect is mimicked in the
   rite: a rain dance may try to cause rain by simulating the sound and pattern of falling drops. Sometimes things used in the rite may work, for
   instance a medicine man may use herbs that have genuine healing powers.
   Arguably technology is magic that works because it has a right understanding of how humanly devised techniques can cause things to happen
   in the world. Thus the rite of two teaspoons of penicillin taken three times
   a day is effective magic for curing 'flu. So for some anthropologists, ritual
   is a primitive form of technology.
3 **Social identity and participation/exclusion** Other anthropologists would
   stress the social rather than the natural effects of rite. Here again the effects

can be real. By doing the same thing together people may be bonded into society. The rites of Sunday lunch and Christmas bind the family together and give it a shared identity. The rites of Remembrance Sunday bind the nation together with ties of patriotic loyalty. Conversely, rites may define who does not belong. Refusal to offer incense to the emperor defined the early Christians as outsiders. In the Balkan wars, Orthodox Serbs and Roman Catholic Croats made the way people made the sign of the cross a matter of life or death. Réné Girard sees ritual as unifying society by creating and sacrificing a common enemy (2001; 2005).

4 **Individual life story – initiation and transition** Ritual can mark the breaking with one community and the joining of another. Typically rites of puberty mark a breaking with the mother-dominated family and a joining the world of adult men or women. This might involve trauma or ordeal to sever the psyche from the former tenderness, and/or the imparting of secret knowledge known only to the new society. Ordination originally marked the joining of the aristocratic order of society; Christians took it over to mark the joining of the clerical community. Marriage in patrilocal society marks the bride's breaking with her family to join that of her husband.

5 **The ordinary** Many rites use the basic things of life: washing and cleansing, eating and drinking together, death (sacrifice), birth or rebirth, sex and fertility. The oldest two professions, priesthood and prostitution, were in many cultures closely linked through temple prostitution, though Judaism and Christianity frowned on the use of down-to-earth sex as a means of communion with the gods (though often happy to use it as a symbol of such union). Obviously weddings celebrate sex, and harvest festivals celebrate fertility in a more discreet way!

6 **The sacred or holy** Finally, a rite may be a sacrifice ('making holy') in which these ordinary things or animals are moved from the human to the sacred order. Typically this involves an offering, in which the humans relinquish ownership of the thing or animal, followed by consecration, in which it is inscribed in the sphere of the holy or divine, typically in the case of animals by slaughter, in which the life-blood is separated and returned to its divine source. Sacred communion may follow, in which humans partake of the food thus made sacred, eating and drinking with

the gods (cf. Exodus 24.3–11, cited on p. 24). But other sacrifices are holocausts, in which the whole animal is burnt and thus consumed by the divine, leaving nothing for the humans. Often such rites atone for sins and restore community between humans and the gods, thus relating to Factor 3.

Exercise

Different groups select a 'rite' from the list 1–9 on p. 4 – say foxhunting or the eucharist – to investigate which of these six aspects might supply the understanding the Martian lacked.

A Three-Dimensional Framework

Note now how these six aspects of rite can be arranged in three 'dimensions' which give a kind of human space in the context of which human rites have human meaning (Figure 1). In this book we shall explore how this space, with modification, can provide a structure to help us understand the sacraments. The bracketed numbers refer to the above list of ways of understanding rites.

- Rites (1) draw on a background of shared myth about the past, but also relate (2) to the future goals and magic ends of those who partake. We symbolize this by a line that really ought to go through the page, from a background that is behind us in the past to a future destination in front of us.
- Rites (3) help to bind communities in which (4) individuals have a place and a story. We symbolize this with the individual, personal and esoteric on the left – the hand used in many cultures for private needs – and the corporate public order of 'right' on the right – the hand we use to greet others and cement social contracts.
- Rites (5) use ordinary matter, full of earthy significance, to evoke (6) a divine or sacred reality. We symbolize this by an arrow reaching downward to the earth, and upward to the heavens.

Figure 1. Dimensions of Rites.

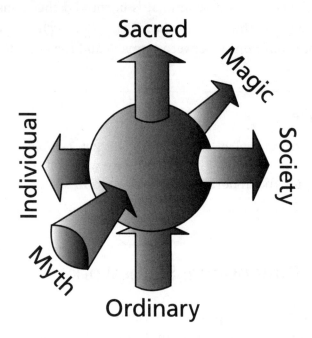

To make this concrete, consider the well-known 'rite' of a birthday party.

- The celebration has been repeated on the same day each year, calling to mind and making real the person's past. Perhaps previous birthdays will be called to mind and retold, or what has happened in the intervening time. But it also expresses hope for the person's future: the sentiment of the Russian Orthodox birthday song, 'God grant you many years', is implicit in every birthday celebration. No doubt the parents hope the party will have a real encouraging future effect on their child.
- This is another year in the individual's life, but the celebration shows that this life matters to a wider community of family and friends, who are gathered and bound together by the event.
- Cakes, candles, games and a meal are ordinary matter, but organized to carry a special enchantment that celebrates the sacredness of the person's life.

Discussion

Can you identify these six elements in a funeral, including both the religious ceremony and the 'do' afterwards as parts of the 'rite'? Also consider: Is it too much to claim that rites are what unite the ordinary and the holy, make us individuals and bind us in community, and give us both our past and our future? Could there be a totally secular society, in the sense of a society without rites?

Further Reading

Tissa Balasuriya, 1995, *The Sense of the Sacramental*, London: SPCK.

Joseph Campbell, 1968, *The Masks of God: Creative Mythology*. London: Souvenir; New York: Viking.

Mary Douglas, 2002, *Purity and Danger*, London: Taylor & Francis.

Mary Douglas, 2003, *Natural Symbols*, London: Taylor & Francis.

Emile Durkheim, trans. Carol Cosman, 2001, *The Elementary Forms of Religious Life*, Oxford: Oxford Paperbacks.

Terry Eagleton, 1970, *The Body as Language*, London and Melbourne, Sheed and Ward.

Mircea Eliade, 1968, *Myths, Dreams and Mysteries*, London: Collins.

Mircea Eliade, 1968, *The Sacred and the Profane*, New York: Harcourt.

Réné Girard, 2001, *I See Satan Fall Like Lightning*, London: Gracewing.

Réné Girard, 2005, *Violence and the Sacred*, London and New York: Continuum.

Roger Grainger, 1974, *The Language of the Rite*, London: Darton, Longman and Todd.

Graham Hughes, 2003, *Worship as Meaning: A Liturgical Theology for Late Modernity*, Cambridge: Cambridge University Press.

Rudolf Otto, 1968, *The Idea of the Holy*, Oxford: Oxford University Press.

Roy Rappaport, 1999, *Ritual and Religion in the Making of Humanity*, Cambridge: Cambridge University Press.

Ross Thompson, 1990, *Holy Ground: The Spirituality of Matter*, London: SPCK.

Victor Turner and Roger Abrahams, 1995, *The Ritual Process: Structure and Anti-structure*, Aldine.

2

Pagan and Jewish Antecedents

In this and the next chapter we will be moving from the general concept of rite to the specific Christian concept of sacrament or mystery. In this chapter specifically we shall explore ways in which the roots of the Christian sacraments may be found in the Jewish religion, which may be called in a broad sense a sacramental faith. There is a paradox about this, however, in that the word 'sacrament' does not appear in the Bible and indeed could not. It is originally a Latin term to which there is no close equivalent in the languages of the Bible: Hebrew, Aramaic and Greek. So we need to begin with an investigation of two crucial terms which the early church took from surrounding pagan culture, but married, as I hope to show, to some very Jewish concepts.

Mysterion

The term 'sacrament' was first used to denote things that had previously been described in Greek as 'the mysteries', though it cannot be said to be a translation of that term since the meanings are quite different. To this day the Eastern churches speak of the 'mysteries' rather than the 'sacraments'. The term has survived in the West too; the 1662 Anglican Book of Common Prayer order for holy communion refers to the latter three times as 'these holy mysteries' and seven times to the 'sacrament'. However, the term is not widely used in the western churches today, perhaps because of the connotations of a sinister puzzle that has to be solved, as in a 'murder mystery', or just something impossible to understand at all. So what did the term originally mean?

The Greek *musterion* derives from *mueo*, to shut the mouth. It denotes a mystery or secret teaching, the kind of revelation that is whispered, passed on to the initiated. It relates to the words *mystikos*, from which we derive the terms 'mystic' and 'mystical'. There is a contrast here with another all-important New Testament concept, *kerygma*, which denotes a message proclaimed abroad to everyone, and relates to the term *keryx*, herald. The contrast suggests that as well as proclaiming a message loud and clear to all, there is a secret, mute, non-obvious, even unspoken communication of the Word of God, passed on perhaps through presence rather than speech. Psalm 19 suggests such a tension between speech and 'no speech' in the Word of God as revealed/concealed in creation:

> The heavens are telling of the glory of God;
> And their expanse is declaring the work of his hands.
> Day to day pours forth speech,
> And night to night reveals knowledge.
> There is no speech, nor are there words;
> Their voice is not heard. (Psalm 19.1–3)

If this is so, then as well as proclamation, theology has to deal with mystery, and a mystical or sacramental theology is needed to balance the systematic and the biblical. The Word of God is both revealed as truth and light, and veiled in darkness in a manner that draws us. Christ is both the epiphany, or manifestation, and for Paul (see next chapter) the mystery of God.

In New Testament times the term had close connections with the mystery cults: secret societies with complex rites involving ritual identification with the gods and goddesses like Orpheus, Isis and Dionysius. Yet it has a mainstream biblical pedigree. The term or its equivalent appears in three major settings, in all of which the concepts of revelation and mystery are interdependent.

The Hebrew *raz* (translated *mysterion*) is used in the apocalyptic books of the Hebrew Bible and Apocrypha, which are full of obscure, dreamlike imagery. *Raz* means something hidden; the imagery conceals a hidden political meaning about the nations and the future, which the prophet reveals. The term occurs eight times in Daniel, mainly in chapter 2 in connection with Daniel's interpretation of King Nebuchadnezzar's dream of the great statue, in which the king acclaims God as 'revealer of mysteries' (Dan. 2.47). It is also found in the Wisdom literature to denote the 'secret purposes of God' (Wisd. 2.22), anticipating St Paul, for whom mystery is closely associated with wisdom.

In the Gospels, *mysterion* appears in Mark 4.11, Matthew 13.11 and Luke 9.1–10, as the secret meaning of the parables. Those outside the kingdom only understand the surface meaning; the mystery is something Jesus shares with the closed 'initiated' circle of his disciples. Here the parables are treated rather like the apocalyptic dreams of Daniel. However, we note that Jesus does not usually treat parables in this way; generally he throws parables at crowds and disciples alike and lets them make of them what they will. Parables are not often allegories in which each thing, as in apocalyptic, symbolizes something else; to grasp a parable we need to look at the story as a whole, and wonder at it. So the esoteric and elitist approach we find on this one occasion perhaps reflects an apocalyptic approach, or the later Pauline theology of mystery, rather than the approach of Jesus himself. This is crucial. Sacraments are much more like parables than allegories. In sacramental worship, we should not look for a hidden meaning to everything (though this is often attempted) but look at the whole picture, and wonder.

For while mystery is rare in the Gospels, marvel is all-pervasive; repeatedly, especially in Mark, disciples and crowds are described as responding to the teaching and practice of Jesus with a range of words that range from wondering (*thaumazo*) through to outright fear (*phobeo*). Such feelings are something we associate with the sacraments. Opinions differ as to whether the mysteries are miracles in the modern sense of overriding nature[1] – I shall argue not – but they are undoubtedly marvels, things to wonder at.

Finally, *mysterion* occurs extensively in the writing of, and that attributed to, Paul. We will return to him in the next chapter.

Sacramentum

A *sacramentum* was in Roman society a pledge of money or property deposited in the temple by parties in a lawsuit or contract, forfeited by the one who lost the lawsuit or broke the contract. It also came to mean an oath of allegiance made by new recruits to their commander and the Roman gods.

Tertullian in c. 210 began a tradition of Latin Christians using this word to denote the acts the Greek-speaking church termed *mysteria*. They were, as the Latin term implied, solemn pledges of allegiance to God. Tertullian preferred the term 'sacrament' because it was free from the pagan connotations of the mystery cults. In Latin the term *mysterium* came to refer to the inner meaning (as in 'the mysteries of faith') while *sacramentum* referred to the outward rite; whereas Greek had only the one word *mysterion* to refer to both. Arguably this later made for a big difference of approach.

Mystery conveys the fact that the act is an outward sign of an inner secret of our relation to God, or as John Chrysostom (1999) put it,

> A mystery is present when we realize something exists beyond the thing we are looking at.

Discussion

Is it appropriate to have mysteries, that is, secrets shared only among the faithful, or should everything be proclaimed to everyone? Do you think Jesus kept some truths only for the disciples, and if so, why?

Theophany and Mystery

So far we have looked at the origins of the concept of sacrament in the older idea of mystery, which only appears in one late strand of Old Testament literature, apocalyptic. But though the specific idea did not loom large, it is arguable that the whole Hebrew vision and practice of its relationship with

God was full of a genuine sense of mystery. This is perhaps best illustrated in the theophanies or experiences of God described in the Hebrew Bible, not least the theophany to Moses in the burning bush. The story (Exod. 3.1–14) is worth reading carefully in full.

We note the presence of all six dimensions:

- God first identifies himself by his saving presence in the past – he is the God of Abraham, Isaac and Jacob.
- But he announces plans for the future – to liberate his people. A translation of the mysterious name at the end is 'I will be whom I will be'; God is saying both that he refuses to be defined in any more limited terms, but is the free God of the future; hence able to liberate people in the present by the limitless power he has shown in the past.
- This is a plan for the whole people, but . . .
- It is directed here through this call to one man, Moses, who at this stage is nobody exalted, but rather a murderer and a refugee, who has found asylum in the wilderness.
- The sacred is clearly present in the holiness of the ground; Moses takes off his shoes, as if he were entering a temple, but . . .
- This holiness is manifest in ordinary matter, in fire and a desert bush, behaving in an out-of-the-ordinary way.

This vision was not a repeated rite, of course, hence not a sacrament, but illustrates the dimensions we expect to be there in the mysteries. A sacrament is a kind of bush burning in holy ground for people's liberation.

Other theophanies worth reading are:

- Jacob's ladder (Gen. 28.11–22), which John's Gospel relates to Jesus lifted on the cross (John 1.51). In discussing the eucharist we shall note the role of the angelic songs and the movements of ascent and descent. Are sacraments a kind of ladder in which heaven and earth become accessible to one another? (Note too the consecration of this early altar, though soon we will encounter an even earlier one.)
- The vision of Isaiah (Isa. 6.1–8). The cherubic song appears at the heart of the eucharist. Orthodox liturgy likens holy communion to the purifying coal pressed to Isaiah's lips.

The Sacramental Word

Herbert McCabe (1964, p. 8) argues that the way the Bible presents not only sacred events but 'sacred history' as a whole is akin to the sacramental:

> In sacred history, then, we have first of all persons, things and events which have a significance of their own, and then their significance is brought out and made clear through the words of Scripture which describe them. As we shall see, in this the Bible resembles the sacraments. In each of the sacraments there is first of all a symbolically significant gesture or thing . . . and then the significance of this is brought out and made clear by words.

The key Hebrew word *dabor*, McCabe goes on to argue, has a sacramental quality as it means both 'word' and 'deed'. God's word, right back to the initial word of creation, 'Let there be light', always leads to a deed or act, and every act or happening in history has a divine word behind it, a divine meaning. In Isaiah 55.9–11 this creative efficacy of the Word is beautifully likened to the way rain makes the earth flourish. The Wisdom of Solomon expresses a similar thought more mythologically:

> While gentle silence enveloped all things,
> and night in its swift course was now half gone,
> your all-powerful word leaped from heaven, from the royal throne,
> into the midst of the land that was doomed,
> a stern warrior. (Wisd. 18.14–15)

This text is used to express the wonder of the 'Word made flesh' on Christmas night. One can certainly see how such a Word might readily become incarnate, and underlie the Christian sacraments; also how wise it is always to include word and sacrament together, and not to set up any false opposition.

The prophets' role was to keep alive this dynamic sacramental unity of Word and act by disclosing the movement of God's Word in historical actions, and conversely to call people to respond to God's Word, thus revealed to them in voice and vision, with actions of justice and faithfulness.

Idols and the Image of God

The Jewish faith has always been deeply opposed not only to idolatry, but to visual representation as such, whether of God or any creature. This is forbidden in the second commandment (Exod. 20.4). And in later prophetic traditions this prohibition sometimes extends to an opposition to the very rituals that earlier traditions had established. In Amos 5.21–24 God is said to despise religious feasts, assemblies, sacrifices and songs, and to want justice instead. In Hosea 6.6 (cited by Jesus, e.g. Matt. 9.13 and 12.7) God says plainly, 'I desire mercy, not sacrifice'.

However, Hebrew tradition does have a positive notion of images, in that human beings are said to be made in the image and likeness of God (Gen. 1.25–26, 5.1, 9.6). The words used here are *tzelem*, a reflection or shadow, and *demus*, something similar, whereas the word for idol is *pesel*, a sculpture, and *temunah*, a precise depiction. So we cannot quite say that images are prohibited because God's likeness is to be found in the human form instead. Nonetheless the thoughts are clearly connected in the minds of the prophets, who do not simply condemn idolatry (and ritualism) but urge something else instead, namely justice and mercy. Instead of worshipping empty forms that cannot contain the reality of God, we should respect one another as the most God-like thing in creation. The notion comes to fruition in the Gospel notion of poor and oppressed people as sacramental of God, so that what we do to the one in need we do to Christ (Matt. 25.40).

The idea that humans image God makes dualism a kind of blasphemy. Hebrew thought never sees human beings as souls in bodies, but rather as a whole sacramental being. Our hands and feet, our senses and our sexual organs, our capacities for thought, feeling and expression, even our hunger and our thirst, image the invisible God and provide, as we shall see, the basis of the sacraments.

To view the rites and sacraments as constituting in themselves images or likenesses of divine reality would be a stark departure from this Hebrew tradition. For Jewish thought such things are always, rather, celebrations of the divine presence, activity and likeness in and among his people.

Discussion

Do you think it is important to understand Christian sacraments in this way? How in practice have they been presented in your experience?

Rites and God's Acts in History

The Jewish faith therefore was and is very focused on the re-presenting of the divine activity through rite. These rites were not static representations of God as object – as in an idol – but dramatic representations of God's Word/action in saving history. This makes a big difference to rite as it exists in Judaism and Christianity, faiths that are anchored in events believed to be part of the people's history.

It has often been noted that 'pagan' rite related to a primordial sacred history. The focus was on myths of creation and their cyclic repetition through the year. The 'future' dimension involved in rite was a repetition of the past; the hope was simply that seed time and rain and sun and harvest would come again, by means of the ritual. It is an exaggeration to say that this aspect was rejected by the Hebrew law and cult. As we shall see, the rites of the great festivals were firmly anchored in the lunar and solar cycles, and make reference to the cycles of growth in the land. The covenant with Noah, whose sign is said to be the rainbow, affirms this so-called pagan, perhaps more properly called 'universal' dimension. However, this repeated cycle is described as being established through a single sacrificial transaction, which does not itself need repeating. So we could say that here the universal natural cycles are themselves established in a linear, 'historical' covenant which makes the regularity of the future different from the flood and chaos of the past.

Then Noah built an altar to the Lord, and took of every clean animal and of every clean bird, and offered burnt offerings on the altar. And when the Lord smelled the pleasing odour, the Lord said in his heart, 'I will never again curse the ground because of humankind, for the inclination of the human heart is evil from youth; nor will I ever again destroy every living creature as I have done.

As long as the earth endures,
seedtime and harvest, cold and heat,
summer and winter, day and night,
shall not cease.' (Gen. 8.20–22)

So the Hebrew rites use natural cycles to express something linear – a past that is not simply a remote golden age, ideal and mythic, from which people had fallen to something mundane and repetitive (though again, there are hints of that scenario in Genesis), but rather, historical. The events that were portrayed with mythical and symbolic vividness were believed to be real events that had shaped a particular people, speaking a creative Word of God that was creating a new, different and better future.

It was in their rites that the Jewish people expressed this dynamic hope. Jewish faith would not call these rites sacraments. It was Christian theologians who called them the 'sacraments of the old covenant', Protestant theologians even insisting on their divine institution and saving character for the Jews. They are in any event essential to an understanding of the Christian sacraments.

Like much worship in the ancient world, Jewish worship centred on sacrifice – the ritual offering of the life of an animal (or a human, but never in the Jewish cult) followed in some cases by its cooking and eating. Like rite generally, sacrifice has been understood in a number of ways. Réné Girard (2001; 2005) has seen it as an act of 'mimetic violence' which holds society together by slaying a common victim. However, this seems to relate most clearly to certain kinds of sacrifice, notably the 'scapegoat' (see below). Others would stress the life rather than the death of the victim, the blood, offered to God, representing the sacred life of the community symbolically offered back to its creator in order that the community may go on living on earth. The immolation (slaying) of the victim is a 'making holy', which is the literal meaning of the Latin term 'sacrifice' – something existing on the mundane level is transferred to the sacred sphere, to open up a channel whereby the community may offer itself to, and in some cases commune with, the divine.

In terms of our three dimensions, the matter–sacred dimension is therefore much in evidence, and there is also a dimension of communion, bringing individuals together in society.

These features are common to sacrifice in world religion; but the difference in approach to time, just mentioned, means that for the Jews the sacred to which the community is lifted exists neither in a remote 'sacred time', nor in an ever-repeated time of the earth, but in historical time, time that opens to a future of difference and hope. This is especially true of the festival rites to which we now turn.

Old Testament 'Sacraments'

I conclude this chapter by inviting the reader to take a close imaginative look at these specific rites. We shall consider the main five feasts through their biblical references, which for convenience are printed out. But remember that (apart from one rite which is described only in the Bible and may never have become a repeated rite) they exist in a modified form (as noted) to this day. If for Christians they are treasured as precursors of the sacraments, for Jews they are precursors of a different tradition, equally alive. Though they have now no temple and no sacrifices, the Jewish people have never ceased to keep these feasts.

Exercise

Complete as much as you can of Table 1. Note that the first month of the Jewish year begins after the spring equinox – call it March – but to complicate matters, Jewish New Year is in the autumn! Where there is no answer an x appears.

Table 1. Jewish Festivals.

Rite	When does it happen?	What is used?	What is done?	What is re-membered?	What is cele-brated or achieved?
Passover					
Pentecost					
Covenant	x				
Tabernacles					x
Day of Atonement					

1 *Pesach* (**Passover**) The people slay a lamb and eat it with bitter herbs, un-leavened bread and cups of blessed wine. Today the sacrificed lamb is absent, replaced by an egg as token of sacrifice, and the expression of hope for return from exile – the hope that wherever the Passover is kept this year, it will be kept 'Next year in Jerusalem!'

> The LORD said to Moses and Aaron in the land of Egypt: This month shall mark for you the beginning of months; it shall be the first month of the year for you. Tell the whole congregation of Israel that on the tenth of this month they are to take a lamb for each family, a lamb for each household . . . You shall keep it until the fourteenth day of this month; then the whole assembled congregation of Israel shall slaughter it at twilight. They shall take some of the blood and put it on the two doorposts and the lintel of the houses in which they eat it. They shall eat the lamb that same night; they shall eat it roasted over the fire with unleavened bread and bitter herbs . . . This is how you shall eat it: your loins girded, your sandals on your feet, and your staff in your hand; and you shall eat it hurriedly. It is the Pass-over of the LORD. For I will pass through the land of Egypt that night, and I will strike down every firstborn in the land of Egypt, both human be-ings and animals; on all the gods of Egypt I will execute judgments: I am the LORD. The blood shall be a sign for you on the houses where you live: when I see the blood, I will pass over you, and no plague shall destroy you when I strike the land of Egypt. This day shall be a day of remembrance for

you . . . You shall observe the festival of unleavened bread, for on this very day I brought your companies out of the land of Egypt: you shall observe this day throughout your generations as a perpetual ordinance. (Exod. 12.1–17)

2 *Shabuoth* (**Weeks of Pentecost**) Seven weeks after Passover, the first-fruits of the harvest are offered and blessed.

You shall take some of the first of all the fruit of the ground, which you harvest from the land that the LORD your God is giving you, and you shall put it in a basket and go to the place that the LORD your God will choose as a dwelling for his name. You shall go to the priest who is in office at that time, and say to him, 'Today I declare to the LORD your God that I have come into the land that the LORD swore to our ancestors to give us.' When the priest takes the basket from your hand and sets it down before the altar of the LORD your God, you shall make this response before the LORD your God: 'A wandering Aramean was my ancestor; he went down into Egypt and lived there as an alien, few in number, and there he became a great nation, mighty and populous. When the Egyptians treated us harshly and afflicted us, by imposing hard labour on us, we cried to the LORD, the God of our ancestors; the LORD heard our voice and saw our affliction, our toil, and our oppression. The LORD brought us out of Egypt with a mighty hand and an outstretched arm, with a terrifying display of power, and with signs and wonders; and he brought us into this place and gave us this land, a land flowing with milk and honey. So now I bring the first of the fruit of the ground that you, O LORD, have given me.' You shall set it down before the LORD your God and bow down before the LORD your God. Then you, together with the Levites and the aliens who reside among you, shall celebrate with all the bounty that the LORD your God has given to you and to your house. (Deut. 26.2–11)

Shabuoth also remembers the giving of the law to Moses on Sinai, and includes a recitation of the ten commandments.

3 *Covenant* Exodus describes the interchange of promises between God and God's people. Gerhard von Rad originated the thesis that there was at one time a repeated 'covenant renewal' ceremony like the other Jewish feasts, though there is no equivalent today.

> Then Moses came and recounted to the people all the words of the Lord and all the ordinances; and all the people answered with one voice, and said, 'All the words which the Lord has spoken we will do!' And Moses wrote down all the words of the Lord. Then he arose early in the morning, and built an altar at the foot of the mountain with twelve pillars for the twelve tribes of Israel. And he sent young men of the sons of Israel, and they offered burnt offerings and sacrificed young bulls as peace offerings to the Lord. And Moses took half of the blood and put it in basins, and the other half of the blood he sprinkled on the altar. Then he took the book of the covenant and read it in the hearing of the people; and they said, 'All that the Lord has spoken we will do, and we will be obedient!' So Moses took the blood and sprinkled it on the people, and said, 'Behold the blood of the covenant, which the Lord has made with you in accordance with all these words.' Then Moses went up with Aaron, Nadab and Abihu, and seventy of the elders of Israel, and they saw the God of Israel; and under his feet there appeared to be a pavement of sapphire, as clear as the sky itself. Yet he did not stretch out his hand against the nobles of the sons of Israel; and they beheld God, and they ate and drank. (Exod. 24.3–11)

4 *Sukkoth* (**Tabernacles**) At the completion of harvest, the people lived outside in tents ('booths') made of branches:

> Now, the fifteenth day of the seventh month, when you have gathered in the produce of the land, you shall keep the festival of the LORD, lasting seven days; a complete rest on the first day, and a complete rest on the eighth day. On the first day you shall take the fruit of majestic trees, branches of palm trees, boughs of leafy trees, and willows of the brook; and you shall rejoice before the LORD your God for seven days. You shall keep it as a festival to the LORD seven days in the year; you shall keep it in

the seventh month as a statute forever throughout your generations. You shall live in booths for seven days; all that are citizens in Israel shall live in booths, so that your generations may know that I made the people of Israel live in booths when I brought them out of the land of Egypt: I am the LORD your God. (Lev. 23.39–43)

5 Yom Kippur (Day of Atonement) A solemn rite to restore broken community between God and his people. A blast on the *shofar* (ram's horn) at New Year announces a ten-day period of penitence preceding Yom Kippur.

And the LORD said to Moses, 'Tell your brother Aaron that he shall not enter at any time into the holy place inside the veil, before the mercy seat which is on the ark, lest he die; for I will appear in the cloud over the mercy seat . . . And he shall take the two goats and present them before the LORD at the doorway of the tent of meeting. And Aaron shall cast lots for the two goats, one lot for the LORD and the other lot for the scapegoat. Then Aaron shall offer the goat on which the lot for the LORD fell, and make it a sin offering. But the goat on which the lot for the scapegoat fell, shall be presented alive before the LORD, to make atonement upon it, to send it into the wilderness as the scapegoat . . . Then Aaron shall lay both of his hands on the head of the live goat, and confess over it all the iniquities of the sons of Israel, and all their transgressions in regard to all their sins; and he shall lay them on the head of the goat and send it away into the wilderness by the hand of a man who stands in readiness. And the goat shall bear on itself all their iniquities to a solitary land; and he shall release the goat in the wilderness . . .' (Lev. 16.2–22)

In current Judaism, of course, there is no goat. A ram's horn (*shofar*) is blown on the New Year to call the people to repentance, introducing a ten-day period of fasting and penitence, leading up to Yom Kippur itself. The day's liturgy begins with the plaintive chanting of the *Kol Nidre*. All rash, unfulfilled vows to God in the past (and in some traditions the following) year are cancelled. Tradition has it that the world is judged each New Year and the decree sealed on the Day of Atonement.

Further Reading

Samuel Balentyne, 1999, *The Torah's Vision of Worship*, Minneapolis: Augsburg Fortress Press.

Margaret Barker, 2003, *The Temple Roots of Christian Liturgy*, London and New York: Continuum.

Louis Bouyer, 2002, *The Christian Mystery: From pagan myth to Christian mysticism*, St Bebe's Publications.

Paul F. Bradshaw and Lawrence Hoffman (eds), 1996, *Life Cycles in Jewish and Christian Worship*, Indiana: University of Notre Dame Press.

Walter Brueggemann, 2005, *Worship in Ancient Israel: An essential guide*, Nashville: Abingdon Press.

John Chrysostom, in Gerald Bray and Thomas Oden (eds), 1999, *1–2 Corinthians: The Ancient Christian Commentary on Scripture*, New Testament, vol. 7, Downers Grove: IVP.

J. H. Eaton, 1981, *Vision in Worship: Relation of prophecy and liturgy in the Old Testament*, London: SPCK.

Eugene Fisher (ed.), 1990, *The Jewish Roots of Christian Liturgy*, Mahwah and New York: Paulist Press.

Herbert McCabe, 1964, *The New Creation*, London and Melbourne: Sheed and Ward.

Tamara Prosic, 2004, *Development and Symbolism of Passover*, London and New York: Continuum.

3

The New Testament: Christ the Mystery and the Mysteries

We have looked at rites in general, and at mystery, theophany, the image of God, and the historically rooted Jewish celebrations and sacrifices. Only now do we have the tools to consider the origins of what Christians would regard as the sacraments proper, in the New Testament. We shall consider these writings in three distinct ways:

- As the primary source concerning Jesus of Nazareth, whom Christians regard as the institutor of the sacraments, and who in any event must in some sense be seen as their source.
- As containing the earliest traditions of Christian sacramental thought, notably in the rather differently sacramental theologies of the Pauline and Johannine traditions.
- Leading on from both of these, as containing the basis of later christological reflections which see Christ as the primary sacrament or mystery.

Jesus and Ritual

Jesus seems to have been ambiguous about ritual observance. On the positive side, according to the Gospel of Luke his family observes the Jewish rites of circumcision and purification very carefully. In John especially, Jesus makes regular pilgrimages to Jerusalem, and teaches in synagogue and temple, as well as attending a marriage feast. All this indicates a respect for the Jewish rites and customs.

Moreover, his healing miracles sometimes involve actions that have a ritual quality. (Read Mark 7.32–35.) Here Jesus' gestures seem designed to cause healing by way of direct contact with the parts that need it, in a way that borders between magic and medicine. However, this is exceptional; Jesus is not normally recorded as using complex gestures, dances, techniques and incantations, despite the prevalence of these in a surrounding culture full of magic and magicians. His wonders rely more on a direct relationship in which faith is invoked, than on an exercise of ritual expertise and power.

Finally, Jesus sometimes welcomes symbolic actions of others. He receives baptism from John. He accepts anointing on the head from 'a woman' (Mark 14.3–9; also in Matthew) and as an anointing of the feet by Mary of Bethany, in John 12.1–8. Such anointing was used for priests and kings, but Jesus accepts it as a preparation for his coming death, maybe as his own priestly offering and kingly triumph. He says that what the woman has done will be told 'in remembrance of her' in a startling parallel to the words at the last supper, 'do this in remembrance of me'. If this were a parallel institution of a sacrament of anointing, the tradition was soon forgotten! Such a darkly playful and paradoxical reworking of the old rites is typical of Jesus, as we shall see.

Jesus Against Ritualism?

Often Jesus' approach to ceremonies is presented as pragmatic rather than ritualistic in the positive and negative senses I have described. He seems to be particularly dismissive of the negative rituals, or taboos. He ignores the sabbath prohibitions in order to heal people and feed himself; he and his disciples ignore cleanliness rules, and (in a passage that possibly reflects later practice of a church that had radically departed from the details of the Jewish law) he declares the food rules redundant. His 'cleansing' of the temple is regarded by some scholars as a symbolic attack on the sacrificial system itself. He is reported by his accusers (Matt. 26.61 and 27.40) as offensively describing his death and resurrection as a destruction and rebuilding of the temple, a theme which Paul may be developing in 1 Corinthians 6.19 when he refers to Christians' bodies as 'a temple of the Holy Spirit'. Certainly his actions in receiving anointing and at the supper suggest he is moving the place of sacrificial rite and the presence of God from the temple building to the human body, especially his own.

So he was creative, rather than obsessive regarding rite, boldly offering his own interpretations and adding his own actions. This is clearest of all in the case of the last supper, where he adds his own remarkable interpretation regarding the bread and wine. In John's Gospel he adds (or substitutes) a footwashing ceremony of his own, which is an ordinary act of service given ritual connotations of cleansing.

In the Gospel accounts and later tradition he thereby instituted a new rite, the eucharist. In Matthew 28.18–end he also institutes a trinitarian baptism. Many would regard this as reading later practice back into Jesus' actions. But it is possible to derive these and some of the other sacraments with more certainty from the example of Christ rather than direct institution (see relevant chapters below on each sacrament). It is certain that he ate food and drank wine with people in an indiscriminate way; almost certain that he was baptized by John (an awkward act for one supposed to be the sinless Son of God, which the Gospel writers would hardly have invented); his healings often involved the laying on of hands; and as we saw, he received anointing.

We may, therefore, characterize Jesus' approach to rites on the positive side as open to existing use and to the rites of others. He was not so much 'against' ritual as non-ritualistic, for he used ritual pragmatically rather than legalistically, in a creative and original, possibly originative (instituting) and certainly exemplary way.

Rites in the New Testament

There is evidence in the New Testament of four regularly used ritual acts:

1 **Baptism** The normal means of admission to the church by profession of faith – at this stage in Jesus as Lord rather than in the Trinity – and a baptismal immersion.

2 **The Breaking of Bread** It is unclear whether this expression is shorthand for a whole meal, or a simple meal just of bread, or what we now term the eucharist with bread and wine.

3 **The Laying on of Hands** A widely used gesture, employed by Jesus as well as his apostles, with an equally wide variety of meanings. Sometimes it followed baptism, sometimes it was independent, and often it was accompanied by a gifting of the Holy Spirit, as for example in Acts 8.14–17 (see Chapter 6). The gesture is also used, by Jesus as well as the disciples, for healing the sick. In fact all the sacraments later associated with this sign – confirmation, ordination, healing – seem to be present in the gesture, but in a less differentiated and regularized way.

4 **Anointing for Healing of Sickness and Forgiveness of Sins** This is prescribed in the letter of James (5.14–15). Anointing of the sick by Jesus' disciples appears in Mark 6.13.

All in all, there was a rich use of rite in the New Testament, but it was all fairly simple and little regularized. We cannot identify the later seven Catholic sacraments straightforwardly, but baptism and possibly the eucharist stand out as present from the earliest times, while we see precursors of the others, with the notable exception of any distinct Christian sacrament of marriage. At this stage it was doubtless normal to accept marriage according to local custom and Roman law.

The Mystery of Christ in Paul

Paul writes about baptism and the Lord's supper, as we shall see when we consider those sacraments. He also uses the term 'mystery' no fewer than 21 times. But he never refers to either rite, or any other particular rite, as a 'mystery'. Nevertheless 'mystery' in Paul is crucial to what would later be called the 'mysteries'. Let us see how.

Exercise

Look at the following passages. Answer:
- Who or what is the mystery?
- What is its relation to time?
- What other ideas is it closely related to in these passages?

1 Now to him who is able to establish you according to my gospel and the preaching of Jesus Christ, according to the revelation of the mystery which has been kept secret for long ages past, but now is manifested, and by the Scriptures of the prophets, according to the commandment of the eternal God, has been made known to all the nations . . . (Rom. 16.25–27).

2 Yet we do speak wisdom among those who are mature; a wisdom, however, not of this age, nor of the rulers of this age, who are passing away; but we speak God's wisdom in a mystery, the hidden wisdom, which God predestined before the ages to our glory; the wisdom which none of the rulers of this age has understood; for if they had understood it, they would not have crucified the Lord of glory; but just as it is written, 'Things which eye has not seen and ear has not heard, and which have not entered the heart of man, all that God has prepared for those who love him' (1 Cor. 2.6–9).

3 With all wisdom and insight he has made known to us the mystery of his will, according to his good pleasure that he set forth in Christ, as a plan for the fullness of time, to gather up all things in him, things in heaven and things on earth (Eph. 1.8–10).

4 Surely you have already heard of the commission of God's grace that was given me for you, and how the mystery was made known to me by revelation, as I wrote above in a few words, a reading of which will enable you to perceive my understanding of the mystery of Christ. In former generations this mystery was not made known to humankind, as it has now been revealed to his holy apostles and prophets by the Spirit (Eph. 3.2–5).

5 I became its servant according to God's commission that was given to me for you, to make the word of God fully known, the mystery that has been hidden throughout the ages and generations but has now been revealed to his saints. To them God chose to make known how great among the Gentiles are the riches of the glory of this mystery, which is Christ in you, the hope of glory (Col. 1.25–27).

In these and similar passages Paul (or perhaps a writer in the tradition of Paul, in the case of Colossians) sets forth the notion that Christ is the mystery, the secret plan of God that has always been implicit in creation, but is now made explicit in Christ. Christ is the predestined mystery of God revealed within the fullness of time. In receiving him, people receive salvation.

The Transfiguration

The synoptic Gospels begin and end with 'mysteries' in Paul's sense: with birth or baptism, and death and resurrection. But at the centre lies the 'mysterious' theophany of the transfiguration (Luke 9.28–36). If we read this with care we will notice the presence of the three dimensions of rite:

- The past is present in the form of Jesus' predecessors, Moses, giver of the law, and Elijah, the archetypal prophet. But they are conversing with Jesus about his future accomplishment of salvation.
- Two fragmentary communities are there: the communion of Jesus with the two past saints, who vanish; and that with the three present saints, who sleep, and then respond – inappropriately, but interestingly enough – by trying to make this event into a ritual, with a hilltop shrine where it can continue to be celebrated.
- Material things – the mountain, Jesus' face and clothes, bright light, and later the dark cloud – become sacramental of something awesome and holy. The Fathers likened Jesus to a new 'burning bush' on the mountainside, lit but not consumed by the divine fire, making the ground holy.

The passage seems to be saying in story form what Paul says theologically, that Christ is the mystery of God through whom we see God's light, the one known long before who will reveal final salvation. In Chapter 5, p. 73 I shall return to look more closely at transfiguration as a way of understanding the sacraments.

Signs in John

Paul's writings include the earliest New Testament writings we have. His notions, with the 'high' christology they imply, had developed certainly within a generation of the death of Christ. The writings ascribed to John are by contrast among the latest such writings, written probably around the turn of the first century. The very oldest people alive then would have only been young children in the time of Christ's ministry. So these writings are generally reckoned to be the fruit of reflection on the experience of the risen Christ in the church, rather than deriving from eyewitness accounts of what Jesus did. Indeed John's Gospel contains very little about what Jesus did; his actions are reduced to a number of signs, and much of the Gospel, at least until the passion, consists of dialogue about the signs.

Remarkably, the sacraments seem to be absent from these writings. Though Jesus is described as coming for baptism (John 1.29–34) the baptism itself is omitted, and we hear only of the descent of the Holy Spirit on Jesus, and John the Baptizer describing him as the one who baptizes with the Spirit. Likewise though a last supper is described, we hear nothing of bread and wine and what Jesus said and did with them, but rather, of Jesus washing his disciples' feet, a story that appears nowhere else in the New Testament. This could be because John's church community had no sacraments, or the writer was anti-sacramental. But if we look closer we can see that the writer is shifting attention from the mysteries to the Mystery, for the way the signs are developed makes Christ himself the sacrament of God.

John's Gospel describes Jesus as the Word of God made flesh (John 1.14), and Jesus repeatedly performs miracles that are signs of his own reality. Typically he follows each sign with a discourse in which he identifies himself with things taken from ordinary life. In this he follows the prophetic tradition we described above, in which the *dabor* or Word of God is always fulfilling itself in deed. In this tradition it makes sense to speak of Word becoming flesh: becoming the sign of God that actualizes his very presence.

- After Jesus feeds the 5,000 with bread and fish, Jesus says:
  'I am the bread of life. Whoever comes to me will never be hungry, and whoever believes in me will never be thirsty' (John 6.35).

And Jesus goes on to speak of the need to eat his flesh and drink his blood (6.53–58).

- While teaching in the temple, and pronouncing forgiveness of the woman caught in the act of adultery, he says:
  'I am the light of the world. Whoever follows me will never walk in darkness but will have the light of life' (8.12).
- When challenged by the Pharisees about his identity, he replies:
  'Before Abraham was, I am.' So they took up stones to throw at him (8.58)
- After healing the man born blind, he declares:
  'I am the gate. Whoever enters by me will be saved, and will come in and go out and find pasture' (10.9) and
  'I am the good shepherd. The good shepherd lays down his life for the sheep' (10.11).
- After raising Lazarus from the dead, Jesus says to Martha:
  'I am the resurrection and the life. Those who believe in me, even though they die, will live' (11.25).
- At the last supper, where the disciples still seem confused about his identity, Jesus says:
  'I am the way, and the truth, and the life. No one comes to the Father except through me' (14.6) and
  'I am the vine, you are the branches. Those who abide in me and I in them bear much fruit' (15.5).
  The latter at least suggests the presence of wine – the 'fruit of the vine' – at the supper and Jesus' identification of himself with it.

We note the recurrence of the words 'I am' in these sayings. Some see this as an identification of Jesus with the divine 'I am', the unutterable YHWH who spoke to Moses out of the bush (above, p. 16). Whether or not this is so, the repetition focuses the Gospel very much on the question of who this Jesus is, an identity that is unfolded through repeated identification with material things that function as signs to something beyond. Through these repeated declarations Jesus is taking material being – 'flesh' – and allowing the divine *dabor* to reveal and real-ize himself through it. Christ is declaring himself as the revelation of the mystery of God, the eternal Word made tangible and visible in material flesh, the efficacious sign or sacrament of God.

Note too that each declaration of identity is followed by an invitation to respond, and an assurance: 'I am x . . . Whoever y . . . will z.' Each sign *invites* a faith (in the sense of a response of commitment) and *leads to* faith (in the sense of assurance) in a pattern that we find all important in the sacraments.

Reflect

There is one exception to this in our list. What do you make of it?

Finally, the writer uniquely describes blood and water flowing from the side of the dead Christ when the soldier pierced his side with a spear (19.33–34). Early tradition understood this as showing the mysteries of baptism and the eucharist flowing directly from the Mystery of the crucified Christ.

In these late writings Jesus is the self-realizing Word of God making created things – bread, light, pathways, life itself, the fruit of the vine, water, blood, breath – into sacraments, effective signs of himself. This notion of the Word of God made flesh in ordinary sign is not far from the thought of those much earlier writings of Paul, which make Christ the Mystery of God revealed in human form.

The Heavenly Sacrifice in the late New Testament

Three late writers contribute a key emphasis to our understanding of the sacraments:

The unknown writer of the letter to the Hebrews puts forward the idea of Christ as the ultimate sacrifice that ends the need for sacrifices. While the old temple rituals had to be repeated because sin and defilement continued, Christ on the cross offered a unique sacrifice in which he was both sacrificing priest and sacrificed victim. This is effective against sin for all time. No longer is there need for ritual as an obsessive repetition; Christian liturgy is a free response to and sharing of the fruits of a perfect sacrifice that has already been accomplished (cf esp. Hebrews 9).

This obviates also the need for special priests to offer sacrifices; the whole people is now consecrated and holy. So 1 Peter 2.9 addresses what may have been a group of newly baptized Christians as 'a chosen people, a royal priest-hood, a holy nation'.

Finally, the book of Revelation (5.6–10) combines both thoughts in its image of the liturgy of heaven. The sacrificed Lamb, Christ, stands as if slain on the central throne, while the presbyters (elders or priests) gather round and offer harp music and incense. The throne shows him as King but it is also the altar of his priestly sacrifice. His royal priesthood spills over to make the whole people 'kings and priests'.

Some believe passages like this reflect the worship of second-century Christians. In any event we find in these three late writers a theology of worship, which has taken the repeated ritual life associated with the priests and the temple (now destroyed) and transformed it through the experience of Christ into the celebratory sacramental life of the whole people. Much in both Catholic and Protestant understandings of the sacraments can be seen as based on these late writers, but while the former justifies, through them, carrying over into the worship of the church the symbolism and ethos of the old sacrificial system, the latter emphasizes the transformation brought about by the event of Christ, rendering sacrifice as such redundant.

The Three Dimensions of the Christian Sacraments

It may help to conclude this section by examining what becomes of the notion of rite in general as it moves to that of sacrament flowing from Christ. We can see that the same three dimensions still hold, but are transformed. (See Figure 2.)

1 The sacraments relate to a specific history of a specific people, the Jews, as told in the *Bible*, for whom many special rites and symbols expressed a special relation with God. As Yahweh, the Hebrew God, had called out his people in past times, Jesus saw himself as calling out a new people;

Figure 2. Dimensions of the Sacraments.

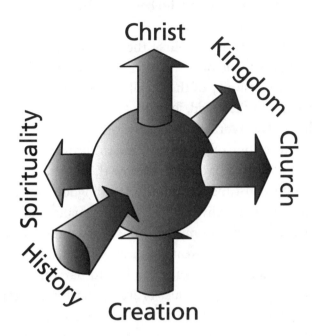

he deliberately used the old calling as the model and context of the new (Wright, 1996).

2 But this history is also told, in prophetic and apocalyptic writings of the Old Testament itself, as well as by the New, as pointing to a future full of both judgement and hope: the *kingdom of God* and the end-time are ultimate values that are so often at odds with those of 'this world'. Sacramental time is the 'between time' between the 'before time' of the Old Testament leading up to Christ and the 'end time' of the kingdom; so sacraments point both ways. The end-time, moreover, implies a final judgement but also the final *pleroma*, a fullness where Christ is 'all in all'; so sacraments all contain a penultimate element of judgement and an ultimate dimension of mercy or loving-kindness.

Because this end is assured by God, and not something the rite causes to happen, the anxious, obsessive striving of magic to achieve a *future effect*, and the obsessive striving of the old sacrifices to please God, give way to a confident opening of the soul to receive something that is already given. If at times the church has relapsed into magical 'works', there have always been those like Luther who have recalled it to the end-time assurance proper to the sacraments.

3 The Christian society is of course the *church*, which both 'makes' the sacraments and is made or constituted by them. In Christian belief the church is the community of those called out of the cosmos (world) but only for the sake of the world, in order to bring the world to the redemption of Christ. The Word and the sacraments between them constitute both God's 'calling out' of the church, and the universal calling of humanity through the church. We shall see how they gather a community that foreshadows the end-time community, the kingdom of God.

4 The life story of the individual is, for Christians and many others, a *spiritual journey*; Christian mystics have charted the journey of the soul to God in ways that draw a great deal, as we shall see, on the sacraments.

5 From a sacramental view nothing can be ordinary or profane. Ordinary matter becomes *creation*, not just brute matter but something God has called into being out of nothing, and which therefore already expresses something of God, as a work of art expresses the artist. An important point (Wink, 1992) which will become clearer as we look at some of the sacraments, especially baptism, is that God creates the cosmos not by mastering an evil and chaotic matter, like Marduk slaying the dragon Tiamat in Babylonian myth, but peaceably, through the speaking of his Word and the breathing of his Spirit over the chaotic 'face of the waters'. Here chaos is integral to the creation, and primal matter is incipiently sacramental, ready for use, as it were, in what we shall term a natural symbolism.

6 The sacred or divine is supremely expressed for Christians, of course, in *Christ*. Institution by Christ is generally regarded as essential to a sacrament, though only for Protestants is this understood as requiring a specific, recorded declaration. More broadly, we have seen that in any case Christ, for Paul, is the primordial mystery and, for John, he unites the divine Word and human flesh, so expressing the invisible Godhead in visible and tangible form. The sacraments then unite the general revelation in creation with the specific revelation in Christ. In traditional terms they unite 'nature' – the created order – with 'grace' – the special gift of God that is Christ.

From this it is clear that sacramental theology needs to study pretty well all the other branches of theology – the Bible, ethics and eschatology, the church, spirituality, the person and work of Christ, and philosophical theology – and has implications for them too. Quite a challenge!

To ponder

Does the three-dimensionality of sacrament suggest trinitarian roots? Suggestions for further thought:

- Rites rely on a hope that the future will be like the past. Good past history is remembered in the hope that good things will happen again in the future. What justifies this hope? We saw how in covenant with Noah God is described as establishing the rhythm and reliability of the seasons. The Father, as source and creator of past and future alike, grounds the existence and the hopefulness of time.

- Rites try to affirm both the spiritual journey of the individual in the context of wider society, and wider society as a healthy matrix in which the individual can flourish. What justifies this loving matrix, and ensures that individuals are not either locked in a competition that destroys society, or overwhelmed by the demands of a totalitarian society or a 'nanny state'? The Spirit, as communion and bond of love, grounds the interdependence of individual and community in the nurturing matrix of 'mother' church.

- Rites assume that ordinary matter can be used to express sacred things. They distinguish the sacred from the profane, but only to reunite them in symbolism. What can justify the distinction and the unity? The Son, as incarnate one, grounds in his person the unity of the sacred and matter, without confusing them, thereby enabling the divine Word to speak clearly through ordinary human things in the sacraments. Neither a Word separated from matter, nor a Word confused with matter, could speak through matter.

Aidan Kavanagh (1981, p. 100) sums all this up in his eloquent description of 'rite', which seems really to be a description of the sacraments and what, for Christians, ultimately validates them:

Rite … is generated and sustained in this regular meeting of faithful people in whose presence and through whose deeds the vertiginous Source of the cosmos itself is pleased to settle down freely and abide as among friends. A liturgy of Christians is thus nothing less than the way a redeemed world is, so to speak, done.

Further Reading

C. K. Barrett, 1993, *Church, Ministry and Sacraments in the New Testament*, London: Paternoster.

P. Berguerrie and A. Loades (eds), 1996, *Christ the Sacramental Word*, London: SPCK.

Christopher Cocksworth, 1997, *Holy, Holy, Holy: Worshipping the trinitarian God*, London: Darton, Longman and Todd. (Useful for later chapters too.)

J. D. Crossan, 1992, *The Historical Jesus: The life of a mediterranean Jewish peasant*, London: HarperCollins.

Aidan Kavanagh, 1981, *On Liturgical Theology*, Collegeville, Minnesota: The Liturgical Press.

C. F. D. Moule, 1989, *Worship in the New Testament*, Cambridge: Grove Books.

Kenneth Stevenson, 1989, *The First Rites*, Collegeville, Minnesota: The Liturgical Press.

Walter Wink, 1992, *Engaging the Powers*, Minneapolis: Augsburg Fortress Press.

N. T. Wright, 1996, *Jesus and the Victory of God*, London: SPCK.

See also under specific sacraments, especially baptism, eucharist and ordination.

Part 2

Developing Theologies of the Sacraments

4

A Very Short History

In Part 1 we have been drawing an ever tighter circle around our 'quarry', the sacraments. We have pursued them first as human rites, second as rites belonging to a particular people, and third as sacraments proper, rooted in the mystery of Christ. And we have suggested how in the sacraments the three dimensions of all rites might be rooted in the threefold nature of the Christian God.

From the New Testament to the Fathers[1]

We saw how the New Testament recorded a great variety of practice we would call sacramental, and a variety of thought about Christ as the mystery and effective sign of God. But there is hardly any detail there about specific rites and how they were performed. With a few notable exceptions, it is not until the fifth century that clear, fixed liturgies and theological reflection upon them emerge. In the intervening period, the existence of 'the mysteries' is assumed, on the analogy of the pagan mysteries familiar in surrounding culture, as when Clement of Alexandria (died AD 215) urged the devotee of the pagan mysteries to come to the true mysteries. The mainstream Catholic Church emphasized the importance of material sacraments, over against Gnostic alternatives which either rejected sacraments in a search for the purely spiritual, or elaborated rites in a complex series of initiations into the ever loftier realms of angels and spirits.

Nevertheless the philosophy to which Fathers like Clement turned to explain Christian faith and the Christian mysteries to the surrounding culture, was that of Plato, for whom the changing material world was a poor expression of a purer, more intellectual and eternal world of ideas or forms. The notion of a mystery – a hidden truth revealed in a material sign or action – lent itself to explanation in Platonic terms, since Platonism effectively made the whole world sacramental of the eternal; every material thing stood for and participated in a deeper spiritual reality. Contrary to some accounts, Platonism thereby affirmed the significance of the material world, but relegated it in a sense to being *only* significant, having its meaning in something more spiritual, more eternal, and in that sense better. Likewise the Old Testament rites could be affirmed, but only as 'types' and 'shadows' of the greater reality to come, which was Christ.

Denys Turner (1995) writes of Christian mysticism as being based on a fusion of two visions. We can perhaps see the history of sacramental theology as a struggle between the two.

- The philosophical vision of Plato, as related in the myth of the cave. We are all prisoners chained facing the wall of a cave, where all we see are the shadows cast by a fire behind us. Like the prisoners, who think the shadows are reality, so we confuse material things with reality, until the philosopher manages to turn round and see the fire, and more than that, break free and ascend out of the cave to see the sun, the source of all light and vision, the Good which Christian Fathers such as Clement and Origen identified with God.
- The vision of Moses at the burning bush, described in Chapter 2: another story with a light, a hero, a turning to see, and a mysterious source, but in a different configuration.

Discussion

What similarities and what differences do you see in these two accounts of the vision of the Good or God? Are either of them a help or a hindrance to understanding the sacraments?

The Seal

Another major contribution to the understanding of the mysteries – many, at least, would argue – came via the development of the New Testament notion of the seal. The New Testament refers several times to a sealing (*sphragizo*), for example in John 6.27, 2 Corinthians 1.21–22, Ephesians 1.13, 2 Timothy 2.19 and Revelation 7.2–3.

A wax seal may ratify a document, protect contents from illicit opening, and/or make clear who the owner is. In the Gospels it is the Spirit who seals Christians to safeguard them for the last day and identify them as belonging to God. The Fathers identified the seal with baptism, and in particular with the anointing that followed it (see Chapter 6). This outward signing was believed to leave an indelible mark upon the soul, protecting and identifying the newly baptized as children of God.

Such notions proved invaluable when the issue arose of deciding when one could rely on a sacrament leaving its mark, and when it might need to be repeated, as in the Donatist controversy.

Augustine: Always Effective, Not Always Fruitful

In the fourth century a dispute arose concerning whether those who had received baptism and ordination at the hands of heretics needed to be baptized or ordained again when they joined the orthodox church; and whether those who had fallen away from faith under persecution needed the same when returning to the fold. Donatus argued that there was one church holding the true faith, so any other body professing a different faith could not be a true church and could not impart true sacraments. A church or its ministers could only give what they themselves had.

Augustine (354–430) retorted by distinguishing between the seal, which was indelible, and the grace, which could be lost by rejection of faith or by sin. The baptismal seal cannot be removed, but the baptismal grace that cleanses from sin could be undone if one sins again after baptism, or abandons baptismal faith. Likewise with ordination: a sinful priest remains a priest, able to minister the sacraments, but his priesthood will not of itself save him from judgement. So sinful or heretical priests and laity do not need to have the seal renewed by rebaptism or reordination, but to have the grace renewed through sacramental penance.

Augustine argued that the sacrament was the action not of the minister but of God. Validity depended not on the grace of the minister but on whether the sacrament is duly performed. Sacraments work *ex opere operato*, by the working of the work itself, rather than *ex opere operantis*, by the work of the worker (minister). All the minister need do is intend, by what he does, to do what the church does, so that the sacrament is properly formed for God to use.

To some ears this sounds like magic, but it is true of any symbol. When I say the word 'cat' it means a feline carnivore not because I have made a special effort to make it mean that (as if I could have made it mean 'dog'!) but because in English that is what those three letters 'c' 'a' 't' strung together mean, and in uttering them I am as it were 'intending to do what the English language does'. In Catholic understanding, the sacraments are the language of God, and as long as we follow that language faithfully and intentionally God will communicate himself through them.

Though sacraments are in this way guaranteed by God, this does not mean that they are automatically effective – or as Augustine would say, 'fruitful' – in people's lives. That depends on the commitment with which we receive them.

Augustine defined a sacrament as 'a sign of sacred reality', and another definition, 'a visible sign of invisible grace', was attributed to him. He distinguished between sacraments of the word: including sermons, prayers, the Lord's prayer, the creed; and sacraments of action, including blessings, the sign of the cross, penitential ashing, oil of anointing, as well as what we term sacraments today.

Western Systematization of the Sacraments

The Eastern Orthodox tradition continued in similar vein to Augustine. Until western influence spread, there was no attempt to limit or define the mysteries. Rather, in the liturgy they proliferated, with the icons and many ceremonies understood as effective signs of the sacred, and the whole cosmos seen as filled with the energies of God. The natural thing to do with the holy seemed to be to celebrate it and let it overflow.

In the West, on the other hand, people tended to make the holy remote, precious and tidy. Peter Lombard (c. 1065–1160) defined the familiar seven sacraments: baptism, confirmation, holy communion, ordination, marriage, penance and extreme unction. Other rites like ashing and blessing were now defined as 'sacramentals'. These were useful symbols but not powerful God-given tools of grace.

One might ask, why seven? Medieval theology had a biblical liking for the number. There were seven days of the week, seven virtues and seven deadly sins. The number was viewed as combining the Trinity of heaven with the four corners of the earth: three plus four made for a deep symbol of unity. In the case of the virtues, the three heaven-given 'theological' virtues of faith, hope and love were added to the more down-to-earth rational classical virtues of prudence, courage, wisdom and justice. No doubt such considerations made people like Lombard keen to find seven sacraments, imparting a satisfying sense of completeness to what could seem – and did seem to Protestants later – a somewhat arbitrary collection.

Lombard (*Sentences*, 4.1.2) also sharpened Augustine's definition in a way Aquinas would develop:

> Something is properly called a sacrament because it is a sign of God's grace, and is such an image of invisible grace that it bears its likeness and exists as its cause.

So sacraments were signs of God's grace in two senses: as a likeness (as a road sign may be a likeness of two old people) and as a cause (as smoke is a sign of fire).

Medieval theology also took over Aristotle's distinction between matter and form. In modern terms we would prefer to speak of matter and meaning or process. We might compare matter to 'hardware' (the actual stuff a computer is made of) and 'form' to software (what a computer does as it manipulates symbols to produce meaningful results). Generally 'matter' was the stuff used in a sacrament – bread and wine, oil, or water – while 'form' was the meaning given by the words said as these things were used – 'This is my body . . .', etc.

Sacramental Reality

In time these somewhat reductionist distinctions were refined into a subtler threefold distinction between:

1 That which is *sacramentum tantum*, only a sign.
2 That which is *sacramentum et res*, both sign and reality, or what is often termed the sacramental reality.
3 That which is *res tantum*, only reality.

In the eucharist, 1) is the bread and wine, 2) is the body and blood of Christ, 3) is union with Christ. In baptism, 1) is water poured, 2) is the baptismal seal, 3) is the grace of regeneration.

Can we make sense of these obscure categories in modern terms? We might use the notion of distinct levels (see p. 72):

1 The material level: what atoms and molecules are doing in the sacrament.
2 The social level: what people are doing in the sacrament through words and signs, which are the way people interact and make a society happen.
3 The spiritual level: what God is doing in the sacrament.

Character

Meanwhile the notion of character, an indelible engraving, or imprinting that leaves an exact copy of the original, was developing from that of the seal. Baptism was seen as creating an exact imprint of Christ, in the sense in which Christ was the exact imprint of God (Hebrews 1.3). And the notion was extended to other unrepeatable sacraments such as marriage and ordination.

Clearly such notions drew on the notion of humanity as being in the image of God, discussed above, though we noted that the word for an exact carved replica was avoided in that context. Character is a kind of sacramental reality, and a modern way of understanding it is in terms of where a person belongs, the society in which she is formed. Through baptism a child objectively belongs to the church so that her very being becomes formed by it; she is 'marked for life'. Through marriage husband and wife 'belong' to one another, and a new society, the family, is generated, in which they will leave their mark on each other and their children indelibly, 'for better or for worse'.

Aquinas: Things that Do what They Say

The key contribution of St Thomas Aquinas (c. 1224–74) was to explain how there could be a 'sacramental reality' that was neither purely physical nor purely spiritual. Though the Aristotelian categories he used are often argued to be outdated, this does not detract from the subtlety with which he brought together real causality and symbolism. Establishing the notion that divine causality can work through human signs, he showed how (in our terms) the divine level can really operate on the material level through the social level of symbolism.

- *The causal dimension*. He regarded God as the efficient cause of grace, while sacraments are instrumental causes; they are God's tools of grace:
    An adze cuts in virtue of its own sharpness, but makes a bed only in virtue of the carpenter's craft; what it contributes to the activity of which it is a tool is its own proper activity; it makes the bed by cutting. In the same way the bodily sacraments, by means of their own action performed on the body they touch, carry out on the soul the activity of which they are God's tool (*Summa Theologiae*, III.62.1, p. 551).
    As tools then, the sacraments contribute their own proper activity to the achievement of God's action in the soul.
- *The symbolic dimension*. But what is a sacrament's 'proper activity'? It is here that we have to introduce the level of sacramental reality. A sacrament is a material thing that God uses effectively for his divine purposes because of its human symbolism. A carpenter could not easily make a bed

with a banana; it would not do what the carpenter needed to do in shaping the wood. But an axe has the sharpness he needs to do the work. The quality a sacrament has which enables God to do his work on the soul is its symbolism.

- This explains the way sacraments work *ex opere operato*. The sacramental action is what God uses to effect grace. The matter of the sacrament therefore matters, because it is not human ideas that God uses, but matter God has instituted as his means of grace. The matter has a natural and human symbolism that renders it usable by God, just as the axe has a sharp shape that renders it usable by the carpenter to produce the bed. Each sacrament is a symbol honed to its task. We will see this more clearly when we consider the individual sacraments.

- This has been summed up by saying that for Thomas, *sacraments say what they do and do what they say*. More fully, they are signs of sacred realities that effect the reality they signify by means of their signifying it within the activity of God (*Summa Theologiae*, III.60.3).

A helpful analogy here is a kiss (Béguerie and Duchesneau, 1980, p. 8):

> A mother who hugs her child does not need to teach it the meaning of this gesture; it springs from love and is understood as such. In this latter case the sign performs an action. It is not content to show love, but brings love alive. It is not just an indication, but makes present what it shows.

There is nothing magic about the way love is communicated and realized *ex opere operato*, in the sheer act of hugging. In the spirit but not the letter of Aquinas we could define a sacrament as a 'holy hug'!

After Aquinas

After Aquinas, the symbol and effect dimensions of sacraments tended to drift apart. Duns Scotus and St Bonaventura regarded sacraments as signs that were the appropriate occasions for God to dispense his grace, rather than integrally linked instrumental causes.

William of Ockham (c. 1284–1347) held a nominalist perspective, that is, for him the meaning or sign aspect of things was an arbitrary human construction. There was no given symbolic order for God to use to make things into sacraments. Bread was just bread, which we could use to signify the body of Christ if we wished.

Other trends emphasized the 'causal' dimension of sacraments divorced from the context of symbolism, in a manner that the Reformation was to criticize as magic and superstition. For example:

- For a long time the sacraments had come to be seen as things, eternally manifesting the things of God, rather than actions signifying and effecting the actions of God in history. This was arguably a move away from the historical perspective of Hebrew rite to a more Platonic view of earthly things as imaging the heavenly.
- People came to mass on Sunday to gaze on the consecrated host, and only occasionally to receive it. The consecrated bread, which had long been discreetly reserved for the sick, was from the Middle Ages in the West housed in a tabernacle on the high altar, where it could be adored. It would be held high in special vessels in processions on Maundy Thursday and Corpus Christi (established in 1264).
- Canon law increasingly applied itself to questions of validity and efficacy to the exclusion of theological issues of symbolism and grace. Sacraments did not have to be 'licit' (properly administered according to the rules of the church) in order to be 'valid' (truly producing their effect). For the latter, only minimal requirements were required. Canon law, like all law, involved 'casuistry', case studies: for example, would dirty water 'work' in the case of baptism; would the bread still be the body of Christ if it were eaten by a mouse?
- On the positive side (Duffy, 2001), medieval society could be said to be built around the sacraments, and in that particular way, around Christ. Christianity was a more popular religion than ever before or since, and arguably superstition and vulgarity were the shadow side of this sacramental devotion. People celebrated Christ in their ordinary lives with great festivity and familiarity, culminating in the great mystery and miracle plays, which were extensions of the liturgy. In the later Middle Ages, after the Black Death, the fear of death and the desire to be assured of heaven became stronger themes.

Summary of the Seven Sacraments

Table 2 summarizes the seven sacraments that are accepted to this day by the Catholic and Orthodox churches. Not all accounts agree, however, on what to put in the three categories, especially in the case of confirmation, penance, anointing and marriage.

Table 2. The Seven Catholic Sacraments.

Sacrament	Approx. date introduced	Material sign	Sacramental reality	Grace effected
Baptism	Easter: 27?	Water in name of Trinity	Character: child of God, royal priesthood	Forgiveness and regeneration
Confirmation	1000	Anointing with chrism or bishop's hand-laying	Character: commitment and worship	Empowering with sevenfold gifts of Spirit
Ordination	200	Bishop's hand-laying	Character: minister of word and sacrament	Pastoral care and faithfulness
Marriage	Pre-history/ 1150	Exchange of vows and rings	Marriage bond	Love and fruitfulness in marriage
Reconciliation or Penance	150	Confession of sins to priest? Or penance imposed by priest?	Reconciliation with church?	Repentance and renewal of life
Anointing for Healing	Disciples' mission: 25?	Anointing with olive oil	Commitment to God's mercy?	Healing of sickness and vestiges of sin, in life or through death
Holy Communion	Easter: 27?	Bread and wine blessed in Eucharist	Body and blood of Christ	Union with Christ

From Sacramental Reality to Relationship in Faith

The Protestant reformers were in continuity and discontinuity with the late Middle Ages. In their sacramental theology we see the continuation of themes found in the medieval scholastics like Bonaventura, Scotus and Ockham, and a continuation of the trend to divorce the significance of the sacraments from their effects. But we find a reaction against the legalism of the canon law approach, and against the late medieval reification of the sacraments.

The reformers believed we are saved by faith alone, and not by works. Luther as a monk had been obsessive and perfectionist in carrying out the 'works' proscribed by the church, but came to feel he had been freed simply to trust in God's love for him irrespective of his shortcomings. This fundamental experience gave rise to a suspicion of obsessive rituals invented by the church, which seemed to represent a human attempt to put ourselves right with God. The reformers rejected any notion that sacraments could cause grace, even instrumentally. The instrumental cause of grace – that which opened the path for God's saving action – became faith, not the sacramental reality itself. And only rites that could clearly be proven to be instituted by Christ were retained. So the sacraments were reduced to two: baptism and holy communion.

Some reformers rejected the term 'sacrament' in favour of 'divine ordinance', though most kept the term 'sacrament'. All, however, emphasized the importance of direct obedience to divine institution, over against the more Catholic notion of relying on the divine institution of the church and 'doing what the Church does'.

The reformers were less interested in the nature of Christ in himself than in what he has done 'for me'. And this was reflected in their sacramental theology: they took less interest in the metaphysics, more in the subjective dimension of what sacraments do for us.

The Reformers' Sacramental Theologies

For the reformers, therefore, the middle term, the sacramental reality, which is both material and spiritual, disappears leaving the outward physical sign on the one hand and the inward spiritual grace on the other. However, for Luther and Calvin (but not Zwingli) the middle term is replaced by the faith of the individual believer, which enables the Holy Spirit to work, making the outward sign fruitful of grace in the soul.

In the Roman Catholic understanding, the faith expressed in the sacraments is primarily that of the whole church, which has a duty to instruct individuals in 'the faith' so they can fully share the benefits of the sacraments. But in the reformers' world this corporate world of symbols has broken down. A chasm has emerged between God and the soul which only God's grace and my personal response of faith can bridge.

Even the reformers, though, would agree with Herbert McCabe (1964, p. 20), that 'we must not think of the response of faith as something that comes from our side to meet the Word of God coming from God's side. The response to the Word is part of the coming of the Word, it is the Word in us.' Calvin especially linked this birth of the Word in us with the work of the Spirit. So the reformers are not as subjective about the sacraments as they sometimes sound to our ears.

However, the reformers were independent thinkers; that after all was one of the points of the reform. Let us look more closely at the varied sacramental understandings of the key theologians.

Luther: Real Presence by Faith

Martin Luther (1483–1546) followed the Franciscan trend of Scotus and Bonaventura in regarding sacraments as reliable occasions (rather than tools) of grace. As a reformer he looked to the plain meaning of scripture rather than deep symbolism, and consequently felt obliged to take literally the words in John's Gospel about eating the flesh of Christ and drinking his blood (6.53–58), and Jesus' identification, 'This is my body . . . blood'.

He believed that a sacrament was a visible sign of an invisible reality, but its power came from God and was released through the faith of the one who received it, rather than through the intrinsic fitness of the sacramental sign. In fact, for Luther (1519) faith was one of the three essential parts of any sacrament:

The first is the sacrament or sign, the second is its significance, and the third is the faith required by these two . . . The sacrament must be external and visible, having some material form; the significance must be internal and spiritual, within the spirit of man; and faith must be applied to use both.

Finally, the bread and wine were the body and the blood in their use in the sacrament, but not in themselves; hence it was wrong to adore them outside the context of the eucharist, as Catholic practice encouraged.

Zwingli: Bare Signs of Salvation

Ulrich Zwingli (1484–1531) denied that sacraments had any particular spiritual efficacy (1981).

Sacraments are simply signs of Christian belief; through them a believer indicates that he belongs to the Church of Jesus.

So Zwingli carried forward the nominalism of Ockham regarding the relation between sign and reality to radical conclusions. For Zwingli, unlike Luther, according to Martos (2001, p. 62):

Faith was an inner experience that no outward sign could cause, and salvation was the direct work of the Holy Spirit who needed no instrumental rite. So sacraments could be no more than external representations of spiritual realities; they did not cause those realities, and they were not needed to become aware of them.

Calvin: A Seal Upon a Promise

John Calvin (1509–64) looked for a middle way between Luther and Zwingli. According to him, sacraments were more than a mere sign but less than a channel of grace. They were, as D. M. Baillie (1964, p. 58) put it, 'a seal set by God upon a promise', making what God has once promised in his Word effective in the present life of the believer, by the power of the Spirit. Interestingly, he uses the rainbow that seals the promise to Noah (see p. 19) to illustrate how material things can bear spiritual meanings in sacraments, clarifying, in response to potential scientific criticism, how the material and spiritual work on different levels (see below, p. 72).

> If any dabbler in philosophy, in order to deride the simplicity of our faith, contends that such a variety of colours is the natural result of the refraction of the solar rays on an opposite cloud, we must immediately acknowledge it; but at the same time we will deride his stupidity in not acknowledging God as the Lord and Governor of Nature, who uses all the elements according to His will for the promotion of His own glory . . . Shall not God be able to mark His creatures with His Word, that they may become sacraments, though before they were mere elements? (Calvin, *Institutes*, IV.xiv.8, 1997)

Calvin restored a trinitarian concept of the sacraments by his emphasis on the involvement of the Spirit, which had been much neglected in the West.

> I consider all the energy of operation as belonging to the Spirit, and the sacraments as mere instruments, which are vain and useless without his agency, but which carry a surprising efficacy when he acts and exerts his power in the heart. (Calvin, *Institutes*, IV.xiv.9, 1997)

This 'surprising efficacy' is very great. If for Aquinas the sacraments were symbolic yet real, for Calvin they were spiritual but real. He could write with intense realism about the body and blood of Christ in the eucharist. Calvin and Aquinas agree in seeing the sacraments as instruments, and ascribing the agency in the sacraments to God. But where for Aquinas they were necessary, instrumental causes of grace, for Calvin they are 'mere' instruments. God can use them powerfully, but he does not need them. It is we who need material signs because of our weak, material human nature; and the weak in faith need the sacraments more than the strong.

Finally, Aquinas' and Luther's sacramental theology seem to take their cue from the incarnation – finding parallels between Christ's taking of material flesh and his presence in the forms of bread and wine – a parallel which the Catholics would make explicit in the Council of Trent (see below). But Calvin's fundamental model seems to be the ascension and Pentecost – Christ is ascended at the right hand of the Father, so he cannot be literally present on earth; but the Spirit lifts us to receive life from his glorified body.

The Roman Catholic Reform

The Roman Catholic Church responded to the Reformation with a reform of its own. In part, this corrected some of the abuses the Protestants had criticized; in part, it reaffirmed the medieval teachings more strongly than before. So in the Council of Trent (1554–64) the gathered bishops reaffirmed the following:

- There were seven sacraments, all instituted by Christ, and together necessary to the salvation of humankind. Not all the sacraments were needed by any individual; obviously we don't all need to marry and be ordained to be saved; but these sacraments are integral parts of God's plan of salvation for humanity. 'Institution' was understood in a broad sense as following the revealed will of God. Trent did not try to prove that Christ had historically instituted all the sacraments in specific declarations.
- The bread and wine of the eucharist disappear to be replaced by Christ, who is present in his body and blood, his soul and his divinity, in both the bread and the wine. Here the medieval understanding of 'concomitance' was upheld: the blood of Christ is present in the outward form of bread as well as that of the wine, and vice versa. This justified the Catholic practice, criticized by the reformers, whereby lay people received only the bread and not the wine; Trent was declaring that they were not in any way 'missing out'. The divinity was present by virtue of the 'hypostatic' (personal) union, whereby Christ unites in his single person both divinity and humanity. Thus, the eucharist is explicitly described in this theology, upheld by Trent, as an extension of the incarnation, or at least analogous to it.

- Devotion to the eucharistic elements was to be encouraged. This developed in time into the service of Benediction of the Blessed Sacrament, as well as silent devotions to the sacrament
- Protestant sacraments were only valid where the intention remained in accord with Catholic teaching. Protestant baptism was valid, therefore, because there was still an intent to make the child a member of Christ's body; but the eucharist was not, because the intention was not to share in the body and blood of Christ, at least as the Roman Catholic Church understood such sharing. The Protestant priesthood likewise was invalid because there was no longer the intention to create priests with the power to offer the body and blood of Christ in the eucharistic sacrifice (see Chapters 9 and 12).

Modern Dualism and the Loss of Sacramental Reality

The last point about the invalidity of Protestant sacraments suggests a reversal of the generous teaching of Augustine regarding heretical sacraments, and a qualification, arguably, of the notion of *ex opere operato*. No longer is the liturgical act itself considered primary, such that those who perform more or less the same rite in their worship must be intending to do what the church does. Rather, the theological understanding of what is done becomes primary. Intention is no longer embodied in the action itself, but concerns ideas one has in one's mind while doing an action with one's body.

We are after all now in the modern period of what the poet T. S. Eliot has termed 'the dissociation of sensibility'. The sacramental and poetic connection between things and ideas that had pervaded the ancient world and the Middle Ages was now, Eliot argued, breaking apart. There was no middle, socially shared ground of symbolic reality. On the one hand, the world of objective matter was increasingly disenchanted of its symbolic significance and 'mechanized', subject to investigation by a fast developing science. On the other, the world of ideas and values was increasingly located inside people's heads and hearts rather than in a beautiful creation. The human person ceased to be a sacramental image of God, and became a mind encased in matter, or in Gilbert Ryle's (2004) memorable phrase, 'the ghost in the machine'. Intentions belong to the 'mind' side of this equation.

Not surprisingly, it was now hard not to speak of the sacraments in a way that sounded either very subjective or very objective. The careful accounts of Aquinas sounded increasingly materialistic in this modern context, while the reformers, often equally careful in their own formulations, were inevitably heard by their more extreme followers and their opponents alike as denying any content to the sacraments beyond the purely personal. Liturgy as an act in which spiritual meaning informed material symbols and gestures in the tacit way it informs human art and interaction generally gave way on the one hand to Catholic ritualism – acts justified by obedience to complex manuals, or by ideas carried in the head that supplied an alleged 'meaning' to the rite; and on the other to Protestant didacticism – a much more restrained liturgy justified by wordy explanations designed to put the right ideas into people's heads.

All was not loss, however. Dualism gave rise to an inwardness as the soul, as it were, grasped its own reality. Relationships that had been ordered by society were now freely contracted into. It was the age of the novel and of romantic relationship, of revolution and the 'social contract', as well as mechanistic science, and we have seen how Protestant sacramental theology emphasized the personal relationship with Christ and the importance of inward scrutiny. Pietism and mysticism flourished, though sometimes divorced from and opposed to doctrine and the structures of the church. Methodism, however, shows how a realist sacramental approach could develop in this new romantic environment, and how 'enthusiastic' piety could make doctrine live in a new way.

In the twentieth century, however, things began to change again. Catholic thinkers recovered the symbolic aspect of the sacraments, and began to use personal and existential ideas to complement the Aristotelian metaphysics used by Aquinas. In many ways Protestant criticism was taken on board without sacrificing Catholic sacramental realism. In the next chapter we consider how theologians – Catholic, Protestant and Orthodox – responded to this new environment.

Further Reading

D. M. Baillie, 1964, *The Theology of the Sacraments*, London: Faber.

P. Béguerie and C. Duchesneau, 1980, *How to Understand the Sacraments*, London: SCM Press.

John Calvin, 1997, *Institutes of Christian Religion*, trans. F. R. Battle, London and New York: Continuum.

St Cyril of Jerusalem, 1978, *Lectures on the Christian Sacraments*, London: SPCK.

Eamon Duffy, 2001, *The Voices of Morebath, Reformation and Rebellion in an English Village*, New Haven and London: Yale University Press.

Mark R. Francis, *Sacramental Theology*, in A. E. McGrath (ed.), 1993, *The Blackwell Encyclopaedia of Modern Thought*, Oxford: Blackwell.

Peter Lombard, *Sentences*. Not in print. Download from www.franciscan-archive.org/lombardus.

Martin Luther, 1519, *Treatise on the Blessed Sacrament and the Brotherhood*, in 1955–86, *Luther's Works*, St Louis: Concordia et al., vol. 35.

A. G. Martimort (ed.), 1988, *The Church at Prayer. Vol. 3: The Sacraments*, Collegeville, Minnesota: The Liturgical Press.

Joseph Martos, 2001, *Doors to the Sacred: A historical introduction to the sacraments of the Catholic Church*, Ligouri, Missouri: Ligouri/Triumph.

Herbert McCabe, 1964, *The New Creation*, London and Melbourne: Sheed and Ward.

Gilbert Ryle, 2004, *The Concept of Mind*, Harmondsworth: Penguin.

Summa Theologiae, vol. 3, quoted from Timothy McDermott (ed.), 1989, *St Thomas Aquinas: Summa Theologiae, a Concise Translation*, London: Eyre and Spottiswoode and Methuen.

Denys Turner, 1995, *The Darkness of God*, Cambridge: Cambridge University Press.

Herbert Vorgrimler, 1992, *Sacramental Theology*, Collegeville, Minnesota: The Liturgical Press.

James White, 1999, *Sacraments in Protestant Practice and Faith*, Nashville: Abingdon Press.

Ulrich Zwingli, 1981, *Commentary on True and False Religion*, Durham, North Carolina: Labyrinth.

5

The Modern Search for the Primordial Sacrament

In this chapter I look at a world recovering from dualism, and as it were trying to put the sacraments together again in a new way. This chapter will focus on different attempts to root the sacraments – in Christ, in the church, and in the whole cosmos – and at criticisms of the resulting views. I end by putting some proposals of my own as to how the mysteries relate to the Mystery of Christ as he remakes the world.

Rahner: Sacraments and Self-transcendence

Karl Rahner restored the notion of symbolic reality by recovering symbols as events rather than static objects. He revived Aquinas' key notion of a sacrament as a symbol that effects the sacred reality it signifies. On this basis he argued that Jesus in his life, death and resurrection was himself the primary sacrament, since these events accomplished the salvation they showed forth.

Traditional Catholic thought had referred to the sacraments as *natural* signs of *supernatural* grace, continuing the incarnation in the way they juxtapose the human and the divine, the natural and the heavenly. But for Rahner the human and the divine were not static metaphysical realms but dynamic. 'Nature' represents not something fixed in us for ever, but what we have achieved so far. The 'supernatural' represents the human urge to go beyond that and transcend ourselves. Sacraments are not static signs, then, but calls to self-transcendence, whose meaning deepens as we grow. Rather than instituting the individual sacraments, Christ instituted a sacramental church: a community that by its sacramental life is ever calling us to move on towards the transcendent mystery of God. These would be key ideas for Schillebeeckx, and for Vatican II.

Schillebeeckx: Christ the Primordial Sacrament

Edward Schillebeeckx (1963) followed up Rahner's notion of Jesus as the primary sacrament, but developed the idea of sacraments as *personal* encounters with God. Love enables us to see the hidden depths, that is, the mystery of another person. In Christ, faith encounters the mystery of God. So Christ is the primordial sacrament who enables us to fall in love with God. After the resurrection the disciples grasped this mystery of God-in-Christ; through entering into his mystery, by the power of the Spirit, they became the Church, itself the sacrament of God.

The sacraments are means by which Christ continues to be sacramentally embodied in the world through his body or embodiment, the church. They reflect seven ways in which the church has chosen to express the mystery of Christ:

- Baptism: his leading into new life;
- Confirmation: his showing of the power of the Spirit;
- Anointing: his healing ministry;
- Penance: his forgiveness of sins;
- Ordination: his ministry to people's spiritual needs;
- Marriage: his faithful love of his bride, the Church;
- Holy communion: his sacrifice of love.

These seven represent a mystery that Christ has instituted in the sense of desiring to hand on to the church. Schillebeeckx believes Christ instituted the inner grace of the sacraments but (in most cases) left their outward form to the church. The church could have developed other ways of being faithful to Christ's institution in this sense, but this is the sevenfold pattern that has evolved and it is a pattern that presents the mystery well. (Perhaps an appropriate analogy here would be translation into English. A poor language user will translate literally, word by word, hanging on to the outward forms of the foreign language, and producing rather stilted English, but a fluent speaker of both will be able to listen for the gist of what a speaker is saying, and then express this 'gist' in fluent English. In the sacraments, Schillebeeckx is saying, the church does not reproduce the outward forms of what Jesus told us to do, but translates the 'gist' of his mystery in its rites.)

Finally, Schillebeeckx affirmed the Catholic teaching that a sign remains a sign of mystery even when not fruitful in the life of believers. Character sets an indelible mark upon the soul, just as a deep human relationship does. After such encounters, we can never be the same again, though whether the encounter leads to good fruit or bad in our life will depend on our response.[1]

Vatican II: The Church as Sacrament

Schillebeeckx was writing at the time of the Second Vatican Council, which explicitly argues that the church is the primary sacrament. The encyclical *Gaudium et spes*, in Article 5, describes the church as 'the universal sacrament of salvation' while *Lumen Gentium* quotes St Cyprian describing the church as 'an indivisible sacrament of unity' (Article 9), and states in Article 1:

> By her relationship with Christ, the Church is a kind of sacrament or sign of intimate union with God and of the unity of all mankind. She is also an instrument for the achievement of such union and unity.

What 'relationship with Christ' establishes this? Article 5 of *Ad Gentes* speaks of the universal commission to baptize and make disciples of all peoples (Matt. 28.18), while *Sacrosanctum Concilium*, Article 5 (following the tradition described in Chapter 3) speaks of the blood and water flowing from the crucified Christ as a birth of the church as sacrament. Most boldly the same encyclical in Article 2 makes explicit the incarnational identity of the church as being 'essentially both human and divine, visible but endowed with invisible realities'.

The Vatican II documents nowhere follow Rahner and Schillebeeckx in calling Jesus Christ the original sacrament, though they establish the church as sacrament from its continuity with Christ, whose sacramental status seems therefore to be implied.

But is it?

The claim that the church is a continuation of Christ is based on Paul's notion of the church as Christ's body. However, this interpretation had already been criticized by Protestant thinkers. Donald Baillie, a Scottish Calvinist, responded (1964, p. 63) to the notion suggested by the Lutheran Oscar Cullmann, that for Paul the church is the spiritual body of Christ, so that Christ continues his incarnation in the church. Here he follows Leslie Newbigin's argument (1960) that the incarnation is not a vague ongoing union of spirit and matter, but an unrepeatable entry of the creator into humanity.

> Incarnation did not go on for ever, but came to an end, and since then the divine Presence is with us in a new way through the Holy Spirit working in the Church through Word and sacraments. That excludes the idea that Christ is actually incarnate in the Church. But of course it also excludes the idea, which sometimes seems to lurk in certain sacramental theologies, that we are concerned with a dead Christ who lived and died long ago and whose grace has to come to us across the centuries as it were through an unbroken sacramental channel. (1964, p. 65)

The second notion here seems to be a caricature of a traditional Roman Catholic understanding – perhaps implicit in the image of the church flowing from the side of the crucified – while the first represents something closer to the new Catholic understanding of Vatican II, but also Cullmann. In contrast with both, Baillie wishes in Calvinist manner to emphasize that Christ is ascended and removed from *historical* incarnation,[2] but present in a new way through the Holy Spirit. Sacraments must therefore start from Pentecost, not from Christmas; from the coming of the Spirit, not from the incarnation. (But to be fair, Vatican II does emphasize the work of the Spirit in creating the church as the body of Christ.)

In any event, the institutions of the church as sacrament urged by Vatican II are open to challenge. Christ in Matthew 28 institutes baptism, of which the church is only the minister, while the flowing of blood and water from Christ, if it is to be understood symbolically at all, suggests the birth of the dominical sacraments, and only thereby indirectly, of the church. So the correct order of institution would seem to be:

Christ > Sacraments > Church

This is different from both the Vatican II scheme:

Christ > Church > Sacraments

and from the Calvinist scheme of Baillie:

Christ > Spirit > Sacramental Church.

Discussion

Which understanding seems most plausible to you?

Modern Orthodox Understandings: The World as Sacrament

Aidan Kavanagh (1981, p. 23) writes, 'cosmology is the foundation on which ecclesiology rests'. But the theologies we have looked at so far say little about the cosmos, despite the fact for the Fathers that the sacraments are firmly anchored in a cosmic Christ who has 'recapitulated' all creation, literally that is, made himself head of it as his body. This is the thought of Colossians 1.15–20, probably an early Christian hymn.

Eastern Orthodox theology never lost this anchoring. One strand of modern Russian thought, running through Vladimir Solovyev, Nicholas Berdyaev and others, suggests a basic identity between the cosmos, the church, Wisdom, and Mary the 'Mother of God'. Jewish thought (for example, Prov. 8) personified Wisdom as a female accomplice of God as he created the world; and there is evidence that some early christologies saw Christ as the divine Wisdom incarnate. Paul, we noted, linked Wisdom closely to the mystery of Christ.

In a different vein, Alexander Schmemann (2002) has argued that the world itself is the primary sacrament. Created by God, the world expresses God's reality such that all things are symbols luminous with God's glory. In the West, Schmemann goes on to argue, the symbolic nature of reality was lost, such that we came to see sacraments as *either* symbolic *or* real. Whereas we saw this 'dissociation' as arising in the late Middle Ages, however, Schmemann sees it as running through the whole of western theology, in its tendency to isolate specific sacraments from their context in the liturgy and in the creation.

If the cosmos is sacramental, why do we need Christ? For Schmemann, it is because of our human turning away from the sacramental receiving and offering of creation, towards a more materialistic, reifying approach. He describes this through the story of Adam, who was given the fundamental 'priestly' calling to name the creatures (Gen. 2.19) and in so doing offer their being, epitomized by the name, back to God. But Adam grasped the forbidden fruit, symbolizing our human tendency to order the world according to our desires rather than their God-given order and meaning. Christ by offering his life and the life of the world back to God 'recapitulates' creation – takes it back into his body under himself as head – and makes it whole and sacramental again. He is not so much the sacrament himself, as the restorer of the cosmos as sacrament.

Again the church is not so much a sacrament or an extension of Christ as the community that continues through its liturgy Christ's priestly offering into wholeness, manifesting the sacramental order of the cosmos. It is not so much a divine–human institution, as the place where the Spirit is accomplishing through our humanity the divinization of the cosmos.

What this 'divinization' (*theosis* in Greek, literally 'godding') might mean is perhaps best expressed in the iconography of the Orthodox Church. Here Metropolitan Anthony Bloom (in Allchin, 1967, p. 40) discusses two Russian icons of the transfiguration, one by Rublev, the other by Theophan the Greek. Each expresses in a different manner the transfiguration of the cosmos in the divine light, or what Schmemann would call the revelation of the world as sacrament:

The Rublev icon shows Christ in the brilliancy of his dazzling white robes which cast light on everything around. This light falls on the disciples, on the mountain and the stones, on every blade of grass. Within this light, which is the divine splendour – the divine glory, the divine light itself inseparable from God – all things acquire an intensity of being which they could not have otherwise; in it they attain to a fullness of reality which they can have only in God. The other icon is more difficult to perceive in a reproduction. The background is silvery and appears grey. The robes of Christ are silvery, with blue shades, and the rays of light falling around are also white, silvery and blue. Everything gives an impression of much less intensity. Then we discover that all these rays of light falling from the divine presence and touching the things which surround the transfigured Christ do not give relief but give transparency to things. One has the impression that these rays of divine light touch things and sink into them, penetrate them, touch something within them so that from the core of these things, of all things created, the same light reflects and shines back, as though the divine life quickens the capabilities, the potentialities of all things, and makes all reach out towards itself. At that moment the eschatological situation is realized, and in the words of St Paul, 'God is all and in all'.

The difference here perhaps reflects a difference of emphasis that runs through the whole tradition. According to one strand, which runs through the prophets, John's Gospel and Protestant theology, God's light is that of judgement, showing up the contrast between light and dark, good and evil, comes to us from outside, and makes us aware that beside the glory of God we can do no good thing. According to the other, running through the Wisdom literature, Luke's Gospel and Orthodox and Catholic theology, God's light shines from the inside of things. God's goodness makes us shine with our own proper goodness, and actually makes us worthy of salvation on our own intrinsic (but of course God-given) merits. In the sacraments, the former tradition has always wanted to make a sharp distinction between God's action and the sacrament itself, while the latter emphasizes how God uses and enhances the intrinsic power of things.

Reflect

Do you find the equivalent of these two icons in the sacraments or the worship more generally? Do they dazzle you with an overwhelming light that makes all clear? Or are they more subtle, restrained and inward, in the way they transform life?

Contexts

The views we have looked at are perhaps not ultimately opposed, but best understood through their living context. Arguably the church as sacrament of the unity of humankind and of human unity with God is best understood in a 'liberation theology' context, where the church struggles through its sacramental life to bring healing, peace and justice to a broken and oppressive world. Here the church is palpably *political* in the sense of being concerned with the human *polis* or city and its struggles. It is, as Aidan Kavanagh argues (1981, p. 42), 'the central workshop of the human city, a city which under grace has already begun to mutate by fits and starts into the City-of-God-in-the-making'.

Of course, many of the radical Protestant churches have often likewise carried this role of supporting the struggles of the poor and crafting a more democratic society. But as Kavanagh (1981) goes on to write, the church is also concerned with the world, the *cosmos*. It is 'the focal point of a World made new in Jesus Christ'.

And the world made new and sacramental through the church's gladness in the risen Christ is perhaps best grasped in the Orthodox liturgy, which never quite ceased to pulsate in body politics that were often in the hands of other ideologies, whether Islamic or communist. There one can almost sense the continuity between the restrained, indomitable joy of the chanting and the cycles of the great feasts, and the liturgy of the stars and planets and the elemental rhythms of life.

Possible Reconciliations

Several factors in the twentieth century have opened up possible ways of rap-prochement between the different sacramental understandings discussed. Above all, the whole ethos of worship in the main churches has changed from ritualism on the one hand and didacticism on the other, to a growing sacra-mentalism that embraces the whole of Christian life. What does this mean?

First, the dualism that has divided us into mind and matter has come to seem antiquated. Many would now agree that we are sacramental unities of body, mind and spirit, made in the image of God, and so need to worship God with our bodies and through material signs, not simply through words and ideas.

Second, we have come to understand rite as an essential dimension of all human life, such that worship should not be ritualistic in the obsessive sense, but will need to contain good rites if it is to relate the whole of our humanity to the whole of God.

Third, there is growing consensus that sacraments are not isolated enti-ties, but living actions working within the context of the whole liturgy or act of worship, and within the whole life of the church.

Fourth, the Holy Spirit, as emphasized in Calvinist and Orthodox tra-ditions, has been recognized as having an essential role in the sacraments. The church does not 'contain' the Spirit but is formed by the Spirit. The sacraments do not flow only from Christ but are trinitarian acts involving the Father as the origin and goal of all worship (and it must never be for-gotten that the sacraments are fundamentally worship), the Son's incarnate presence and institution, and the Spirit's faith-imparting and community-building action in the church and world of today.

Fifth, massive changes in Roman Catholic thought have reintegrated the sacraments into the life of the church and God's whole work of salvation, whether or not one accepts the Church as the primary sacrament. Indeed, ongoing differences over the sacraments probably now reduce to differences over the Church – whether or not one sees it as a divine–human continua-tion of the incarnation, or a Spirit-gathered but essentially fallible human institution.

Finally, we have seen that for much of Christian history discussion around the sacraments has been polarized, first by the divergence between the Orthodox East and the Catholic West, and then by sharper controversies between Catholic and Protestant. The latter has pitted a 'high' view of church and sacrament as the arena of salvation against a view that would see salvation in terms of a direct relationship between Christ and the believer, expressed and perhaps supported but never mediated through the church and the sacraments. But in modern times a wider variety of differing perspectives has flowered in all traditions, such that there is probably as much controversy within denominations as between them. Indeed many of the high-level inter-denominational agreements seem to have left the old polarities behind, just as at grassroots level sacramental sharing is increasingly common; it is the middle ground of synodical discussions and liturgical revision that sometimes seems to be stuck in sixteenth-century categories.[3]

In this new, non-polarized theological space, it is possible to shed new light on the relation of the sacraments to Christ and the church. Let us see how.

Christ as the Primordial Mystery of God

The problem now becomes whether we can reconcile these views:

- Everything in the cosmos is sacramental.
- Christ is the original sacrament.
- There are particular sacraments in the church.

Discussion

What do you think?

Here is a suggestion:

1 Everything speaks of God. If God is the infinite source of finite beings, Aquinas argued, God must possess qualities analogous to the qualities of beings, but infinitely greater. The psalms and Wisdom literature are clear that the cosmos expresses God, rather as a work of art expresses its creator. Psalm 19 moves readily from the laws of nature to the moral laws

of God (see also Pss. 104, 139 and countless others). Now a painting, if not a self-portrait, is not a likeness of its maker. But all the energy in the brushstrokes and the feeling expressed must have some analogue in the mind of the artist. That is how we can tell a Van Gogh from a Rembrandt. Likewise the universe tells us something of the mind of its maker. It is a visible, physical thing that expresses the ineffable, spiritual God. In that loose sense it is the sacrament of God.

2 However, there is reason to be wary of the attempts of some cosmologists to deduce 'the mind of God' from observation of the universe. For, though we believe the world is the expression of God, we do not understand God's language. This is beyond our rational powers to work out, partly because our minds are darkened and confused by sin, partly because we only see a fragment of the whole cosmos, and partly because human beings can fully understand only human minds, human language and human art. It is as if we are in a dark room gazing at a small fragment of a painting and trying to fathom the mind of the artist.

3 But in Christian belief, in Christ the Word of God speaks through a human tongue, and expresses in his life the whole of God. It is as if the artist himself entered the room and explained the picture to us. Christ gives us himself as the language to understand what God is saying in the cosmos. To see him as divine is to see all things as lucid in his light, as sacramental, God-communicating.

4 But Christ is not bodily present with human beings now. The specific mysteries (sacraments) are those material actions and things that communicate his presence in the here and now. They are not places where we exclusively locate the mystery of God, but things that enable humans to touch and partake of Christ as God's mystery, such that the whole of life becomes sacramental of God. Or to return to our painting analogy, they are paintings God goes on painting through our hands; the more we go on painting, the more we grasp the mind of the artist, manifest not only in the sacramental painting, but in the whole work that the universe is.

The sacraments or mysteries, then, are particular acts that focus the whole mystery of Christ as the mystery that is the life of the Church and its members, and ultimately the life of the world.

Before we move on, the reader may be questioning how a material thing can convey a mystery at all. How can it both be what it is – say water in baptism, or wine in the eucharist, physical things our physical bodies touch – and something else – the means whereby God touches the soul, as it were? If this is a difficult idea for you, the next section may help. But if the reader finds the idea is natural, it may be preferable not to complicate things with too much philosophical reflection, but to skip the following section.

Levels and the Sacramental Reality

How can there be a 'sacramental reality', something that is at once symbolic and real? How can something both be itself and express another reality?

Things exist on different levels. For example, I can describe the hitting of a cricket ball as:

- part of an overall strategy by a cricket team;
- an action by the batsman;
- a set of contractions in the batsman's arm and leg muscles, leading to movement of the bat and ball;
- the movement of elementary particles and forces following laws of nature.

All the descriptions may be valid on their own level. What a commentator must not do is mix levels. If he said,

> ... and now we see the English strategy coming into full force, causing the batsman's nerve endings to make his arm contract, generating a collision between the molecules in the bat and those of the ball ...

the commentator would be using language at all four levels just described all at once, creating an incoherent description. It is the same with sacraments. The three things described by Catholic theology as the reality, the sacramental reality, and the sign, may be understood as actions taking place on different levels:

1 The ultimate level of divine grace operating in the church.
2 The sacramental level where realities like character, and the body and blood, operate.
3 The physical level of doing things with bread, wine, water, etc.

And Protestant theology and Schillebeeckx make clear another level that is always involved:

4 The personal level of the encounter with Christ in faith.

So in baptism something happens on all four levels, simultaneously:

1 The divine action whereby God redeems his church from the waters of death through Christ's death and resurrection.
2 The sacramental action where the individual is indelibly marked out by a particular society, the church, as belonging to Christ dying and risen.
3 The physical action of immersing the person in, or pouring on, water.
4 The personal journey of the individual to repentance, faith and commitment.

These four things may all be happening on different levels and not necessarily simultaneously. The act of God may be once for all, the sacramental action and its physical expression once for all (as in baptism) or repeated (as in the eucharist), and the personal journey zigzagging and confused (see Chapter 7).

We can call Christ the sacrament of God because these same four levels operate in him. For example in the transfiguration, already discussed, we see:

1 The act of God, declaring Jesus his Son, against the background of the law and the prophets.
2 The sacramental transfiguration, as Christ becomes bathed in divine light.
3 The physical elements: mountain climbing, clouds descending, sleep and waking. Possibly a detached onlooker would have seen nothing other than such things.
4 The personal journey of Jesus, wrestling on the mountain, perhaps, with his dark future destiny on the cross; and the disciples, humanly mystified by this mystery.

Different people focus on different levels. With the sacraments, as with Jesus, only the eye of faith can discern the deeper levels.

On this account we can see the church too as sacramental because of these four levels. The church is all of these things:

1 A divine organism, the body of Christ.
2 A worshipping organism, celebrating the cosmic liturgy including the sacraments.
3 A fallible human institution.
4 The place where Christians come together to express, confirm and nourish their personal faith.

Different traditions emphasize different aspects, but if we accept the idea of levels, they need not clash. Ideas only clash if they are on the same level. For example, something cannot be a square and a circle because these terms describe incompatible kinds of the same level of thing, that is, shapes. But nothing prevents a thing being square and red, say, or a cricket bat and a collection of wood molecules, or divine and human, because these terms describe different levels.[4]

Finally, all-important to a sacramental theology is how we treat the relationship between levels and reality. There are three possibilities:

• *Reductionism* The view that only the lower levels have reality, the 'higher' or 'deeper' ones being fictions or constructions built out of the lower level 'bricks'. Margaret Thatcher was being a kind of reductionist when she famously said that there was no such thing as society, only individuals. Certain scientists are reductionists when they say there is no such thing as an individual, only atoms. On such a view sacraments could only be fictional constructions, perhaps stimulating our imaginations or doing us good, but in no way putting us in touch with levels of reality larger than ourselves.
• *Platonic Realism* The opposite view, already discussed, whereby the 'higher' levels are the most real, and the lower ones mere shadowy reflections. On this view sacraments put us in touch with a reality that is already there. The lower reality is made transparent to the higher. At consecration – on such a view – bread and wine fade away before the greater reality of the presence of Christ.
• *Emergence* An intermediate view. As with reductionism, the higher levels are constructed from the lower, but as with Platonism, the higher levels

are real. A higher level 'whole' emerges out of the coming together of lower level 'parts'. So when atoms come together in a certain way they form life, a new kind of reality which needs to be described in a new kind of way. Likewise, when living cells come together in a certain way they form a human body. And when human beings come together in certain ways, they form dances and symphonies and parliaments and festivals and so on – all kinds of social reality. On this view the sacraments would constitute the emergence, as human beings come together in a certain rite-based social way, of a higher level of reality, the body of Christ. Aristotle provided an early theory close to emergence, when he turned Plato's immaterial and static forms into patterns that are always tied to matter, which is forever dynamically realizing its potential in new and higher forms. Many scientists are now exploring more sophisticated versions of emergence, though other scientists are reductionist and a few are Platonist.[5]

We can see how theology has explored all three of these ways of understanding the sacraments. For some traditions they are 'nothing but' human signs, for others they are matter becoming transparent to the eternal, and for yet others, matter and society realizing themselves in new ways in interaction with God.

From the Mystery to the Mysteries

If Christ, the church, the sacraments and the cosmos all have a sacramental nature, operating on different levels in the way just described, how do they relate to one another? And in particular, how do the sacramental mysteries flow from the mystery of Christ?

Inspired by Schillebeeckx, I make the following suggestions (see also Figure 3):

1 Jesus' life was the *outward manifestation of an inner power* that was at once that of God humanized and humanity redeemed and made divine. His power was renewing, spiritually enabling, healing, reconciling, kingdom-proclaiming, loving, and self-offering. I place Jesus, manifesting these powers, displaced from the centre to show that this life was limited to one space and time.[6]

Figure 3.1. Jesus' Life.

Figure 3.2. Jesus' Death.   Figure 3.3. Church Born of the Spirit.

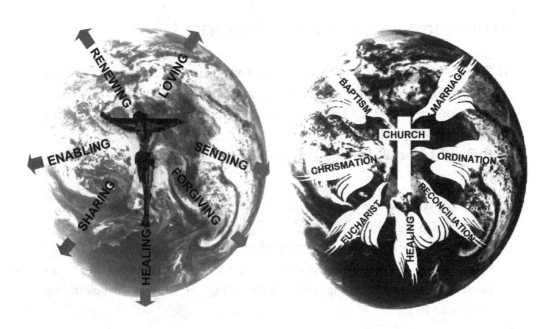

Figure 3.4. Fruitfulness in Life Today.

Figure 3.5. The World and the Kingdom.

2 In death and resurrection this *inner mystery was released outward* to become available to his followers. The dark 'mystery' of human evil flows into the wounded head, hands and heart of the dying Christ.[7] The holy, sacramental mystery of God flows out from the dead Christ. This is one traditional way of approaching the 'atonement'.

3 The Spirit raises Christ from death and *makes the personal life of Jesus the corporate life of the church*, shared through the seven sacraments of baptismal renewing, spiritually confirming, anointing for healing, reconciling of penitents, kingdom proclaiming, marital loving, and eucharistic offering. Sacraments are realities of the Spirit, part of the new creation whereby God gives his Son back to the world which crucified him, for its eternal life. They are shown as dovelike tongues of fire flowing in upon the world to create the universal church.

4 At the same time the Spirit makes this corporate *new creation of the church the personal life of the believer*, so that the participant who welcomes the Spirit's inner work is not only marked with Christ's reality (character or seal) but has this reality revived and rendered fruitful in the believer as it comes to bear just those inner fruits and powers that Christ had: renewing, spiritually enabling, healing, reconciling, kingdom proclaiming, loving, self-offering. Here we see women and men restored to Christ's image and engaging in the life the sacraments have formed in them.

5 But this personal transformation serves the transformation of society into the kingdom. The inner fruits of the spirit are meant to flow outward again to consecrate the world and prepare it for Christ's final coming, when he will be all in all, as the figure tries to show. Thus Thomas Aquinas related the seven sacraments to aspects of society, and following his general intent though not his detail, we could suggest that:

- Baptism consecrates birth and life itself, but also death and loss as the way to new life in Christ. It celebrates 'natality' – humble joy in the gift of life itself.
- Confirmation consecrates childhood, learning, nurture, education and all that enables people and gives them courage and confidence to grow.
- Holy communion consecrates our social nature: friendship, festivity, eating and drinking together, and our political life.

- Reconciliation consecrates, not sin itself, but sin repented of and forgiven, as well as systems of law and justice, as a way to fuller and more honest life.[8]
- Healing consecrates pain, sickness, failure and disability, as well as hospitals, therapy and medicine, as paths to wholeness.
- Ordination – when understood collaboratively – consecrates everyone's work, vocation, achievement and service as a 'sending' or mission by Christ in the world. And finally
- Marriage consecrates joy, sex, love, desire, procreation and creativity.

This list shows how sacraments can provide a yardstick for how society measures up to the kingdom of God. We can judge a society by the way it honours life, educates, shares and celebrates, reconciles and restores through its justice system, cares for everyone's health and well-being, ensures people have good, properly rewarded work, and protects authentic sexuality, family life and children. But the sacraments are also means by which we become the sort of people who will help make a society that does these things well.

Moving back to ecumenical issues, these suggestions enable us to agree with Catholics that sacraments are real instruments of grace, but with Protestants that they are spiritual and Spirit-created realities, rather than continuations of the incarnation through the church. For the purpose of the sacraments is not to reveal a miraculous presence within the church, but to form, inform and transform the church, its members and ultimately the whole world.

Further Reading

A. M. Allchin (ed.), 1967, *Sacrament and Image: Essays in the Christian understanding of man*, London: Fellowship of St Alban and St Sergius.

Anglican-Roman Catholic International Commission (ARCIC), 1978, *The Three Agreed Statements*, London: CTS/SPCK.

E. J. F. Arndt, 2004, *The Font and the Table*, London: James Clarke.

D. M. Baillie, 1964, *The Theology of the Sacraments*, London: Faber.

John Hick, 1977, *The Myth of God Incarnate*, London: SCM Press.

Aidan Kavanagh, 1981, *On Liturgical Theology*, Collegeville, Minnesota: The Liturgical Press.

Joseph Martos, 2001, *Doors to the Sacred: A historical introduction to the sacraments of the Catholic Church*, Ligouri, Missouri: Ligouri/Triumph.

Leslie Newbigin, 1960, *The Reunion of the Church*, London: SCM Press.

Catherine Pickstock, 1998, *After Writing: On the liturgical consummation of philosophy*, Oxford and Massachusetts, Oxford University Press (a difficult book!).

Susan A. Ross, 1998, *Extravagant Affections: A feminist sacramental theology*, London and New York: Continuum.

Edward Schillebeeckx, 1963, *Christ the Sacrament of the Encounter with God*, London and Melbourne: Sheed and Ward.

Alexander Schmemann, 2002, *For the Life of the World: Sacraments and Orthodoxy*, New York: St Vladimir's Seminary Press (originally published in 1966 by Darton, Longman and Todd as *The World as Sacrament*).

Ross Thompson, 1990, *Holy Ground*, London: SPCK.

Patricia Wilson-Kastner, 1999, *Sacred Drama: A Spirituality of Christian Liturgy*, Minneapolis: Augsburg Fortress Press.

World Council of Churches, 1982, *Baptism, Eucharist and Ministry*, Geneva: WCC.

Valuable websites as of September 2005 are:

www.catholicdatabase.com/?page=councils contains statements of all Catholic Councils, including Vatican 2.

www.wcc-coe.org/wcc/what/faith/bem1.html World Council of Churches site linking to all the texts of *Baptism, Eucharist and Ministry*.

www.warc.ch/dt/erl1/ 'Semper Reformanda' (World Alliance of Protestant Churches) site linking to a variety of interdenominational dialogues.

Part 3

Becoming Church: Sacraments and Christian Initiation

6

Evolution of Baptism and Christian Initiation

In this part we examine the way sacraments have marked the process of Christian becoming. Central to all traditions is baptism, which will be our main focus, but we shall also consider other rites that have been used to mark stages of the process, notably confirmation or chrismation, which Catholic and Orthodox traditions regard as sacraments. This chapter will focus on historical developments, while Chapter 7 will draw out the important issues of how we celebrate baptism and Christian initiation today.

Origins of Baptism

Most rites, baptism included, draw on what we may call a 'natural' symbolism, that is, what a thing means simply in the context of the needs and desires of humans as living organisms (cf. Mary Douglas, 2003, *Natural Symbols*). Water is a powerful natural symbol of:

- *Cleansing* Many land-living animals wash in water, humans included. Religions that focus on ritual or spiritual purity frequently use rites of washing to signify and effect cleansing from sin or impurity. This can become obsessive, as depicted by Shakespeare in Lady Macbeth's guilty imagination of blood on her hands, which she tries repeatedly to wash off. But for most people it is important to wash at the beginning of the day, and this probably always has a ritual aspect of washing away the darkness of the night and the chaos of dreams, enabling us to feel good about the coming day. Hinduism merely extends this when it makes ablution at the beginning of each day mandatory. Many faiths, including Islam, prescribe washing before entering a place of worship; the stoup of holy water at the entrance of Catholic churches, and the sprinkling at the beginning of the old Catholic mass, provide for token, ritual cleansings of this kind. Up to New Testament times, the ascetic monastic community of the Essenes used frequent ablutions for cleansing, and John the Baptist baptized in the Jordan for the washing away of sin in preparation of the righteous remnant for the last day.

- *Life* Especially in dry lands, water is essential to the life of crops, animals and humans. Water is a sign and agent of regeneration, refreshment, life and restoration. Wells and springs are widespread symbols of life and healing. The garden of Eden was watered not by rain but by a 'mist' or 'flood' (Gen. 2.6) which divided into four rivers (Gen. 2.10–14), probably recalling the Mesopotamian origins of the Israelites in a land where irrigation was necessary for life. The book of Revelation describes the New Jerusalem as a new Eden, the river of life 'bright as crystal' flowing from God and the Lamb, with healing trees growing on its banks (Rev. 22.1–2).

- *Death* In the winter of 2004, the Asian tsunami reminded us of the primeval power of water. Water and storms can destroy and drown. The stories of Jesus and the disciples in the storm on Lake Galilee reflect this. The Israelites feared the ocean as the place of primal chaos from which dry land had been formed. It was in water that God had all but destroyed the world in Noah's time (Gen. 6–9) – a story that again reflects origins in Mesopotamian lands that became flooded as the Ice Age receded and ice-caps melted.

For the Israelites these meanings were, as noted, written into their history. For them, water was also a symbol of transition – the crossing of the water of the Red Sea, and later, the Jordan, on the way to freedom and the promised land.

These experiences of water were also written back into the first origins, where God is said to create out of a 'formless void' and 'the face of the deep' which is also 'the face of the waters'. Water here carries the meaning of death – a dark, lifeless, brooding chaos before creation – but also life – a womb of potential which the *ruach* (wind, breath or spirit) and the *dabor* (word) fill with light, and later, life (Gen. 1.1–5).

The Baptism of Christ

> The beginning (*genesis*) of the good news of Jesus Christ, the Son of God . . . In those days Jesus came from Nazareth of Galilee and was baptized by John in the Jordan. And just as he was coming up out of the water, he saw the heavens torn apart and the Spirit descending like a dove on him. And a voice came from heaven, 'You are my Son, the Beloved; with you I am well pleased.'
>
> And the Spirit immediately drove him out into the wilderness. (Mark 1.1, 9–12)

This passage and its equivalents in the other Gospels are decisive for the understanding of Christian baptism. Many of the points take up the 'natural' themes of cleansing, life and death:

- It is, as the opening verse declares, a *genesis*, a creation. Like the first creation, we note, it involved the watery deep, the Word of God and the Spirit. So for Christians, baptism is a new creation, new life.
- It includes John's *baptism of repentance and cleansing* from sin, though here Christians believing Jesus to be sinless encounter a problem. It is similar to the later problem of why we baptize innocent babies.
- As well as the creation, Jesus' baptism *recapitulates the fall*. Christians often answered the problem just stated by seeing Jesus as humbly identifying with sinful humanity as he later would on the cross. Note too that the Spirit 'immediately' drives him out into the wilderness. Immediately after recapitulating the creation he recapitulates the fall, when Adam was driven out of Eden (Gen. 3.22–24). If we apply this to Christian baptism, we will have to see it likewise as an identification of the baptized with humanity in its sin and desolation, as something Christ has taken to himself and

restored to God. It will be an act of commitment to the destiny of humanity as fallen and saved, as one is 'drowned' in the waters and then 'rescued'. This is not a theme Christian tradition has dwelt on, but we will see that it is a fruitful one to develop.

- It is a *trinitarian theophany*. *Christ* appears publicly; indeed, John and Mark do not bother to tell us anything about Jesus' earlier life. The *Spirit* appears in tangible form for the first time. The voice of the *Father* is heard addressing the Son in whom he delights. Christian baptism soon came to involve profession of faith in the Trinity, and immersion in the name of the Trinity. Arguably the baptized themselves are a new 'theophany'.
- The *dove* may suggest the dove that returns to Noah when the floods recede, underlining the theme of new beginning and a covenant with all creation (see Chapter 2). But there are other interpretations.
- The baptism *inaugurates Jesus' earthly ministry*. For Christians, as affirmed by Protestants and by Catholics at least since *Lumen Gentium* of Vatican II, baptism is initiation into the 'royal priesthood' of Christ.
- Especially when read in the context of Paul, this 'beginning' of the Gospel *prefigures its end*, the descent into the waters signifying Christ's death, the 'coming up' his resurrection and ascension, and the descent of the Spirit Pentecost. Jesus is described (Mark 10.38) as referring to 'the baptism that I am baptized with', meaning his coming crucifixon, while John the Baptist describes Jesus (Luke 3.16) as the one who 'will baptize you with the Holy Spirit and with fire', referring to the end-time outpouring of the Spirit at Pentecost, and perhaps the fires of judgement.

In a long line of recent scholars, including Oscar Cullmann, Geoffrey Lampe argues (1951, p. 6) that Jesus' baptism is the model for all Christian baptism. If so, it is neither a profession of faith previously attained, nor a rite needing completion in subsequent profession of faith and gifting with the Spirit at confirmation:

> The descent of the Spirit upon Jesus at His baptism was a descent upon us because of His bearing our body; and it happened . . . for our sanctification, that we might share his anointing. Every baptism administered according to Christ's ordinance . . . is linked to our Lord's baptism in Jordan

... Christian baptism is the application to each believer of the baptism of Christ as it was consummated and fulfilled in His death and resurrection. The Christian who has sacramentally died and risen with Christ to the new life in the Spirit is 'anointed in the Messiah' upon whom the 'unction' of the Spirit came, and through whom the Spirit was poured out.

Baptism for Paul

For Paul, baptism is first and foremost participation in the death and resurrection of Christ, bringing new creation.

> Do you not know that all of us who have been baptized into Christ Jesus were baptized into his death? Therefore we have been buried with him by baptism into death, so that, just as Christ was raised from the dead by the glory of the Father, so we too might walk in newness of life. For if we have been united with him in a death like his, we will certainly be united with him in a resurrection like his. (Rom. 6.3–5)

Baptism joins us to the body of Christ, which is a universal new humanity in which all share equally regardless of race, gender or status (1 Cor. 12.12–13). Baptism is a 'putting on' of Christ (possibly a reference to the rite of putting on a white garment after baptism):

> For in Christ Jesus you are all children of God through faith. As many of you as were baptized into Christ have clothed yourselves with Christ. There is no longer Jew or Greek, there is no longer slave or free, there is no longer male and female; for all of you are one in Christ Jesus. (Gal. 3.26–28)

Paul also speaks of the 'seal' in reference to baptism – see Chapter 4 above. Some see this as a distinct rite of anointing or laying on of hands to impart the Spirit, prefiguring confirmation. But Lampe argues forcefully that it was baptism itself that was said to impart the seal, arguing from the integrity of baptism and the descent of the Spirit in the accounts of the baptism of Christ.

Baptism in the Gospels

Other than the momentously significant baptism of Jesus, there is little reference to baptism taking place in the Gospels, apart from two isolated, late references to Jesus and/or his disciples baptizing in John 3.22 and 4.2.

In the great commission in Matthew 28.16–20, Jesus' words 'make disciples of all nations, baptizing them in the name of the Father and of the Son and of the Holy Spirit' are generally cited as Jesus' institution of baptism. However, this passage is unique to Matthew, and the trinitarian formula suggests that later practice is being projected back onto Jesus, since as we see next, the references in Acts refer to baptism in the name of Jesus.

Finally, John's Gospel describes Jesus telling Nicodemus that 'no one can enter the kingdom of God without being born of water and Spirit' (John 3.5). Jesus is describing the need to be 'born again' or 'from above' (*anothen*). Though some Christians relate this to a spiritual conversion, the reference to water in conjunction with the Spirit suggests baptism. So Jesus' evocative words about the wind/spirit (*pneuma*) need to be applied to the life of the baptized:

> You must be born from above. The wind blows where it chooses, and you hear the sound of it, but you do not know where it comes from or where it goes. So it is with everyone who is born of the Spirit. (John 3.7–8)

Baptism in the Acts of the Apostles

The Acts of the Apostles refer to a great variety of baptisms of individuals, households and entire crowds (cf. in addition to the passages below, Acts 2.37–42, 10.48 and 22.16).

Exercise

Read the following passages and note what happens in terms of
- instruction or preparation;
- follow up;
- relation to Holy Spirit.

(Philip has been preaching in Samaria with very positive results.)
When they believed Philip, who was proclaiming the good news
about the kingdom of God and the name of Jesus Christ, they were
baptized, both men and women . . . Now when the apostles at Jerusalem heard that Samaria had accepted the word of God, they sent
Peter and John to them. The two went down and prayed for them
that they might receive the Holy Spirit (for as yet the Spirit had not
come upon any of them; they had only been baptized in the name of
the Lord Jesus). Then Peter and John laid their hands on them, and
they received the Holy Spirit. (Acts 8.12, 14–17)

(An Ethiopian eunuch has been reading Isaiah and seeing Philip,
asks him to explain the passage.)
'About whom, may I ask you, does the prophet say this, about himself or about someone else?' Then Philip began to speak, and starting with this scripture, he proclaimed to him the good news about
Jesus. As they were going along the road, they came to some water;
and the eunuch said, 'Look, here is water! What is to prevent me
from being baptized?' He commanded the chariot to stop, and both
of them, Philip and the eunuch, went down into the water, and Philip
baptized him. When they came up out of the water, the Spirit of the
Lord snatched Philip away; the eunuch saw him no more, and went
on his way rejoicing. (Acts 8.34–39)

(Saul has just been converted – and blinded – by his vision of Christ
on the Damascus Road.)
Ananias went and entered the house. He laid his hands on Saul and
said, 'Brother Saul, the Lord Jesus, who appeared to you on your
way here, has sent me so that you may regain your sight and be
filled with the Holy Spirit.' And immediately something like scales
fell from his eyes, and his sight was restored. Then he got up and
was baptized, and after taking some food, he regained his strength.
(Acts 9.17–19)

(Paul discovers a group of Christians at Ephesus, and says . . .)
'Into what then were you baptized?' They answered, 'Into John's
baptism.' Paul said, 'John baptized with the baptism of repentance,
telling the people to believe in the one who was to come after him,
that is, in Jesus.' On hearing this, they were baptized in the name
of the Lord Jesus. (Acts 19.3–5)

Baptism is clearly the best attested sacrament in the New Testament, but we learn remarkably little about how it was done. John's baptism of repentance is distinguished from Spirit-imparting Christian baptism, but it appears that the Spirit could be given, before or after baptism, by laying on of hands. Acts 2.38 and 10.48 refer to baptism 'in the name of Jesus', while the terms *bapto* and *baptizo* mean dipping in water; probably the earliest form was a single immersion after profession of faith in Jesus as Lord.

Acts refers several times (e.g. 16.15, 16.33, 18.8) to the baptism of whole households together. This would probably refer to children and slaves, with the head of the household having authority to make decisions for the whole house. But there is no direct reference to infant baptism in the New Testament.

Development of the Catechumenate

These New Testament references to baptism are fairly informal and flexible in pattern. But in the first centuries, prior to Constantine, under persecution, the church was in many ways forced to be a secret society. Baptism became increasingly elaborate.

By the fourth century, we can reconstruct the following fairly consistent and universal pattern, the main structure of which, to judge by Tertullian and Hippolytus, was broadly in place by the beginning of the third century.

- *Catechumenate* After an initial enquiry as to suitability, the candidates would be enrolled as catechumens. Certain professions, from soldier and gladiator, through actor and idol-maker, to pimp and prostitute, would have to be given up. A sponsor would vouch for the character of each catechumen and act as his or her guide. As much as three years of instruction in the Christian faith followed, including exorcisms to deliver the candidates from the demonic effects of idolatry and false worship, as well as extended periods of fasting. Much of this was done in secret, because of the dangers of persecution.
- *Enrolment* for baptism. Forty days before Easter, the bishop would enter the names of the candidates in a book. This led to a period of instruction,

the learning of the Lord's prayer and the apostles' creed, intensive prayer, fasting and further exorcisms. This period is the origin of Christian Lent.

- *Vigil* All this culminated in a vigil (recently revived in the Catholic and many other churches) through the night leading into Easter day. In the darkness of the night the paschal candle would be lit from the new fire, symbolizing the light of the risen Christ. With the congregation the candidates would listen to readings about the antecedents of baptism: God's Spirit moving on the waters as the world was created, the flood and the covenant with Noah, the exodus through the Red Sea, and Ezekiel's vision of dry bones being clothed in flesh and coming to life.

- *Baptism* At first light the candidates were taken to a special place, a baptistery or a pool, where they were stripped naked by the deacons and deaconesses (men and women being baptized separately for decency), and the whole body anointed with olive oil, rather as one would before bathing in the Roman baths. The devil and his army of angels, his enticements, and all his works were in turn renounced (in the Eastern church this was said addressing the devil, facing the still dark western sky) and a threefold covenant with Christ undertaken (often said turning to face the dawn in the East). The water was exorcised and blessed, and each candidate was immersed in the water three times, after professing faith in first the Father, then the Son, then the Holy Spirit.

- *Chrismation and robing* The sign of the cross was made on the forehead, usually with chrism, a mixture of olive oil and fragrant balsam, symbolizing entry into the royal priesthood of Christ the Anointed One, and in the East, the gifting of the Spirit. Sometimes all the senses, and the hands, breast and feet, were chrismated. Sometimes the feet were also washed as a symbol of the calling to serve and as a reminder of Christ's service to his disciples. The candidates were then dressed in a white garment – the origin of our 'christening gown' – viewed as a wedding dress of marriage to Christ, or as the Pauline 'putting on' of Christ already referred to. This would often be worn for the whole of the 'bright week' following Easter. In the western church, the bishop then laid hands on the neophytes (newly baptized), sometimes sealing their foreheads with oil, and prayed for their receiving of the Spirit with his seven gifts of wisdom, understanding, counsel, might, knowledge, faith and the fear of God (based on Isaiah 19.3).

• *Participation in the Easter eucharist* The neophytes were often given lanterns or lit candles with which they processed back into the church, newly aflame with the risen Christ. There they shared for the first time in the prayers of the faithful and in the eucharist. Sometimes they were given milk afterwards as a sign of entry into their 'promised land', or of their being 'newborn babes' in the faith. Their initiation was at last complete.

All this might be criticized for losing the original simplicity of New Testament baptism. But clearly here was a church for which the coming of a person to faith was seen as central to the church's task, requiring a careful co-operation with the grace of God through the teaching and rites that preceded and accompanied the great sacrament. In an early case of 'inculturation', the church used the language of the mystery cults, with which the candidates would be familiar, to draw them deep into Christ.

Exercise

Imagine yourself undergoing the above process. What would your feelings about it be? In what ways would it have helped or hindered you in your spiritual journey?

Baptism of Infants and its Rationale

The above process clearly regards adult baptism as normative. Indeed because of its awesome nature, and because at most one repentance was allowed after baptism, baptism was generally deferred to adulthood, or even to late in life, to avoid the risk of damnation through post-baptismal sin. But there was a contrary trend to baptize babies, especially in North Africa. We noted the uncertainty regarding the children of households in Acts, but by 200 CE children were certainly being baptized.

The baptism of adults clearly emphasized repentance of sin, exorcism from evil and profession of faith, but what could this mean for a baby who knew no right or wrong and could profess no faith? Here Augustine stepped in to define the position that became normative in the West, arguing that the infant inherited an 'original sin' from Adam, passed down from generation to generation through the sinful, lustful act by which we are all conceived. So the child needed baptism to free it from original sin. If it could not profess faith, this could be done on its behalf by its sponsors or godparents, in the hope that it would grow up to believe this faith.

Discussion

Do you think these notions of original sin and professing faith on another's behalf, make sense?

Note that it was not the doctrine of original sin that encouraged the practice of infant baptism, but vice versa. Many western theologians regard original sin as a crucial Christian doctrine, but it entered into Christian thought for strange reasons, and is still not accepted by the Orthodox.

Augustine made another, less well-known change. According to then prevailing theology, the water blessed by the priest became the instrument of the washing of the Holy Spirit. This was analogous to holy communion, where the priest would consecrate the bread and wine to become the instruments of grace. But Augustine argued that what conveyed the Spirit was not the substance of the blessed water, but the action of baptizing, whereby the Spirit stamped the seal of Christ on the believer's soul. In emergency, a layperson could baptize so long as it was with water in the name of the Trinity.

Initiation in the Eastern Tradition

In the East the pattern described in detail above continued to be the norm, but increasingly the norm for infants rather than adults. Because the bishop had blessed the chrism, he did not need to be there for the chrismation itself. However, the sequence was compressed into a single week, or even a day, though first communion would be deferred until the child could receive the bread and wine. The process was viewed as a complete initiation into the church.

Augustine's account of original sin was rejected. On Orthodox understanding, we inherit a damaged human condition which needs healing through baptism and the other sacraments, but only the conscious choosing of evil can be regarded as sinful. So later, as awareness, choice and hence sin became possible, penance was required before holy communion. Hence in Orthodox churches holy communion is often received only by children and by those preparing for death by regular confession, though efforts are being made in many areas to restore a more general communion.

Though part of a single liturgical sequence, the 'sealing' with chrism after baptism came to be regarded as a mystery in its own right. So in an Orthodox view:

- *Baptism* cleanses people from sin and joins them to the one body of Christ. It is related to the paschal mystery of the death and resurrection of Christ.
- *Chrismation* seals the newly baptized, imparting the Holy Spirit more personally to the believer. All the senses are sealed, so that whatever the child experiences in life will not be corrupting, but interpreted by the inward sense of the Holy Spirit. The mystery is related to Pentecost, where the separate tongues of fire signify how the Spirit comes uniquely to each believer, creating a part of the one body with its own unique gifts (cf. Schmemann, 1976, pp. 103–8).

The theology of the East, which distinguishes the work of the Spirit more clearly from that of Christ than does the West, is apparent here.

Baptism in the Western Middle Ages

In the West there was much more of an attempt to rationalize and simplify these ceremonies, adapting them to practical need. Baptism at first retained its place as part of the Easter mysteries, but the rite was reduced to three exorcisms on the preceding Sundays. There was provision for a very simple emergency baptism for sick infants. By the eleventh century this was becoming the normal form of baptism.

Because of the number of babies needing to be baptized, instruction and the bishop's involvement were deferred. Thus anointing and laying on of hands for the Spirit's gifting became a separate rite of confirmation (see below). First communion became another separate occasion. Total immersion, which remained the norm in the East, was slowly replaced by the pouring of water over the head; baptisteries ceased to be built; fonts stood at the entrance of the church, and as the Middle Ages progressed, were built smaller, since total immersion was no longer practised.

This was the somewhat minimal rite Aquinas describes in his theology. For him, the 'matter' of baptism was water, poured, while the 'form' consisted of the words, 'I baptize . . . in the Name of the Father and of the Son and of the Holy Spirit.' Baptism imparted an indelible *character* which predisposes the child to receive grace in the form of the theological virtues, faith, hope and love, and the spiritual gifts which would be conferred at confirmation. So faith was not a prerequisite of baptism, but a gift that baptism prepares one to receive.

Confirmation

We noted that the laying on of hands was a frequent New Testament sign of the gifting of the Spirit, sometimes following baptism, sometimes denoting conferral of authority, and often accompanied by charismatic signs like speaking in tongues. Though the sign is the same as western confirmation, the rite is too variable in the New Testament to be viewed as its prototype.

In the West, it was felt necessary to retain the bishop's direct involvement through laying on of hands, so the rite became separated from baptism for the pragmatic reason that the bishop could not turn up at every baptism. Initially confirmation took place at the earliest opportunity, but in the twelfth to thirteenth centuries there was a shift to puberty. As a result, theologians have never been very clear in what sense the Spirit is given at confirmation as distinct from the giving of the Spirit. The word 'confirm' means 'strengthen', and the rite was generally seen as a kind of 'booster dose' of the Spirit, giving one courage to confess Christ publicly. Aquinas relates baptism to 'spiritual birth' and confirmation to 'spiritual growth'. Though the seven spiritual gifts cited above (on p. 91) belong to confirmation, Aquinas does not suggest that the Spirit as such is not given till then.

In current Roman Catholic practice the rite of confirmation is a rite of commitment at variable ages. However, since 1910 first confession and first communion in the Roman Church have generally taken place at the age of discretion, when one is old enough to tell right from wrong, at about six years old. Confirmation has tended to take place later, often at puberty, though there is no rigid rule, and Leo XIII commended the practice of confirmation before first communion. The sacrament can now be administered by a priest through chrismation, as in the East.

In some understandings, confirmation is viewed as a kind of enrolment in the 'lay apostolate' – the time when the Christian, having received her faith from others, takes responsibility for passing it on, and is gifted with the Spirit for this task. In other churches, similarly, confirmation has been seen as a paradoxical 'ordination to the laity'. Though the sacrament has certainly been linked to courage for mission, such an 'ordination' does not seem to be the official teaching of any church.

In the Anglican and many Reformed churches confirmation is normally celebrated at the onset of puberty, sometimes later, to allow for an adult decision. The Church of England still in practice sees the rite as part of initiation, and therefore required before communion, though elsewhere in the Anglican Communion, and now in experimental areas in England, holy communion is allowed before confirmation, as in current Catholic practice.

However, this remains controversial. Some argue that adult commitment and understanding are vital in order that the confirmed can 'discern the body' and receive the benefits of communion. Others insist that children, having been united to the body of Christ and receiving the Spirit at baptism, should be treated as full members of the church. Others yet again argue for an 'open table' at which all who love the Lord are welcome to receive holy communion; on such a basis children can hardly be excluded.

In the East, we noted, chrismation is temporally continuous with baptism, but theologically sharply distinguished from it. In the West, the temporal distinctness between baptism and confirmation is greater, but the theology is less clear. Indeed it has been termed 'a rite in search of a theology'.

Discussion

1 Which of the various theologies of confirmation/chrismation – if any – strike you as most plausible?

2 At what age do you think confirmation/chrismation should be administered: along with baptism, at puberty, in mature adulthood, or never? Can you justify your view from your answer to 1)?

Baptism for the Reformers

Luther regarded baptism (like communion) not as an instrument of grace in itself but as guaranteed effective by the Word of God when received by faith; for 'the power, effect, benefit, fruit and purpose of baptism is to save'. By faith Luther meant not so much intellectual assent, as a heartfelt response of trust and personal commitment to God's promises. We need a rebirth that is both by baptismal water and by spiritual regeneration or conversion – rebirth of 'water and the Spirit' (John 3.3) . Infant baptism is therefore valid, but remains dormant until, as an adult, the person makes a response of faith. Here Luther distinguishes what constitutes baptism from what enables us to receive it (Large Catechism of 1529, p. 53).

Calvin regarded salvation as predestined for the elect, so baptism could make no real difference. However, like good works in general, it was a valuable if fallible sign that one was of the elect, appropriate for true believers and their children. Baptism, he argued (*Institutes*, IV.xv.1):

> is given to us by the Lord as a symbol and a token of our purification . . . It is like a properly witnessed legal document in which he assures us that our sins are cancelled and blotted out, so that they will never appear in his sight or come into his memory or be charged against us.

The Westminster Catechism, published by the Calvinist Puritans at the time of the Civil War, regards baptism as a real conferral of the Spirit, but in chapter 28.6 separates the time of the giving from the sacrament itself (see below, p. 104):

> The efficacy of baptism is not tied to that moment of time wherein it is administered; yet notwithstanding, by the right use of this ordinance, the grace promised is not only offered, but really exhibited and conferred by the Holy Ghost, to such (whether of age or infants) as that grace belongeth unto, according to the counsel of God's own will, in his appointed time.

Zwingli regarded baptism as a visual reminder of how God saves us – through the death and resurrection of Christ – but not as having any relation to the state of grace of the particular people baptized.

Anabaptists and Baptists applied the Calvinist understanding of baptism as a sign of salvation already accomplished, by insisting on believer's baptism. Only when assured of the faith that receives grace should the believer profess that personal faith by being baptized. The baptism is a sign of the faith he or she believes, and the salvation he or she is assured of.

The Anglican Book of Common Prayer in Article 27 retained a Catholic view of baptism as a sign and instrument of regeneration that effects what it signifies:

> Baptism is not only a sign of profession, and mark of difference, whereby Christian men are discerned from others that be not christened, but it is also a sign of Regeneration or new Birth, whereby, as by an instrument, they that receive baptism rightly are grafted into the Church; the promises of forgiveness of sin, and of our Adoption to be the sons of God by the Holy Ghost, are visibly signed and sealed; Faith is confirmed, and Grace increased by virtue of prayer unto God. The baptism of young Children is in any wise to be retained in the Church, as most agreeable with the institution of Christ.

This last 'institution' may be referring to Jesus' laying hands on children (Matt. 19.13–15). His insistence to his disciples, 'Let the little children come to me' is often used in support of infant baptism, though of course Jesus was not baptizing children in this case!

Baptismal regeneration – the view that people are spiritually 'reborn' by means of baptism – came to be challenged in the Church of England. Evangelicals either assigned the rebirth to the moment of conversion rather than baptism, or argued that regeneration at baptism was conditional on the faith of the recipient; while rationalists wanted to resist a 'magic' view of baptism. Baptismal regeneration was reasserted by the Oxford Movement, but in 1850 the evangelical Gorham was upheld by the courts, which declared that the 'conditional understanding' was compatible with the teaching of the Church of England.

In recent times the Church of England's *Common Worship* has restored a full baptismal liturgy with the possibility of a catechumenate-style staged process of instruction and initiation, and additions to canon law have emphasized the importance of instruction for parents of infants being baptized.

Meanwhile *Catholicism* from Trent onwards has condemned these Protestant variations while affirming the validity of Protestant baptism. The importance of teaching the faith through catechism was emphasized.

Much *ecumenical agreement* has recently been reached on baptism, not least the recognition of each other's baptisms as making genuine Christians! In its agreed statement on *Baptism, Eucharist and Ministry* ('BEM' for short), the World Council of Churches, which includes the Protestant and Orthodox churches but not, as full participants, the Roman Catholics, affirms a great deal about baptism under the following headings:

- Participation in Christ's death and resurrection.
- Conversion, pardoning and cleansing.
- The Gift of the Spirit.
- Incorporation into the body of Christ.
- The sign of the kingdom.

More about BEM in the next chapter.

Summing Up

The Christian churches divide along three fault lines:

1 **How to baptize** For Orthodox and Baptists – otherwise often at opposite extremes – baptism is necessarily by total immersion, while all the others allow pouring as the norm.

2 **Who to baptize** For Anabaptists and Baptists, baptism is the believer's expression of (accomplished) faith in God; whereas for all the others, it could almost be described as God's expression of faith in the (future) believer. The former therefore only baptize believers, while the latter baptize children, though increasingly admitting only the children of believing parents.

3 **What baptism does** For Calvin and Zwingli it is only the sign of a regeneration that takes place independently, whereas for (most) Lutherans, Anglicans, Catholics and Orthodox, it is an effective sign imparting a genuine regeneration, Christian character and membership of the church, though this will only bear fruit when the baptized develop their own Christian faith.

Discussion

Which of these views do you identify with? Is it God's faith in us that baptism expresses, or our faith in God, or both?

Further Reading

Baptism

John Calvin, 1997, *Institutes of Christian Religion*, trans. F. R. Battles, London and New York: Continuum.

Anthony R. Cross, 2000, *Baptism and the Baptists: Theology and practice in twentieth-century Britain*, London: Paternoster.

Mary Douglas, 2003, *Natural Symbols*, London: Taylor & Francis.

Joachim Jeremias, 1960, *Infant Baptism in the First four Centuries*, London: SCM Press.

Joachim Jeremias, 1965, *The Origins of Infant Baptism*, London: SCM Press.

Aidan Kavanagh, 1978, *The Shape of Baptism*, New York: Pueblo.

G. W. H. Lampe, 1951, *The Seal of the Spirit: A study in the doctrine of baptism and confirmation in the New Testament and the Fathers*, London: Longmans, Green.

Martin Luther, 1955–86, *Luther's Works*, St Louis: Concordia.

R. R. Osborn, 1972, *Forbid Them Not: The importance and the history of general baptism*, London: SPCK.

Alexander Schmemann, 1976, *Of Water and the Spirit*, New York: St Vladimir's Seminary Press.

Confirmation specifically

James Behrens, 1995, *Confirmation: Sacrament of Grace*, London: Gracewing.
Dom Gregory Dix, 1946, *The Theology of Confirmation in Relation to Baptism*, London: Dacre.
Aidan Kavanagh, 1988, *Confirmation: Origins and Reform*, New York: Pueblo.
Michael Perry (ed.), 1967, *Crisis for Confirmation*, London: SCM Press.
L. S. Thornton, 1954, *Confirmation: Its place in the baptismal mystery*, London: Dacre.

7

Sacraments, Stages and Society: How Should We Make Christians?

In this chapter we take up two areas of concern related to those reached at the end of Chapter 6:

1 *How* Christian initiation should be carried out. Whether by a single sacrament of baptism, a combination of baptism, confirmation and first communion, or a longer stage-by-stage 'catechumenate'.
2 *Who* baptism should be administered to. All who ask, believers and their children only, or mature believers only.

Both areas of concern raise theological issues of how one becomes a Christian, and what baptism does; whether it is a complete initiation or needs completing or complementing in some way by confirmation or other rites.

In addition, both areas of concern open up wider issues:

Area 1 raises the issue of the relation of sacraments to spirituality and the stages of life.
Area 2 raises the issue of the relation of sacraments to society, and whether ultimately they 'belong' to the church or the wider world. How we practise baptism will depend on and focus how the church sees its own relation to the world. The theology of Richard Niebuhr will give us some concepts to articulate these relations.

Finally we shall consider some practical case studies that will help us relate all the above issues to pastoral situations.

Sacraments and Stages

It is very common for societies to mark stages in people's lives by rites of initiation or transition. Most widespread of all are the rites that mark the end of childhood and the entry into adult society. Often adolescents will be taken out of their homes and made to live in isolation from their families, undergoing painful and frightening trials and ordeals, as well as instruction through myth and ritual, before being readmitted to society as adults. (In many ways such a process remained intact in the British public school system until quite recently!) In a sense they are helped to 'die' to childhood and its security and 'rise again' to new life as adults. Adolescents still often feel a need to withdraw from home life into their own world and their own often chaotic and trauma-inducing 'youth culture' before emerging into adulthood, and some argue that the difficulties many face in negotiating their journey through adolescence into adulthood may be related to the lack of structured initiation rituals and practices in our own society.

Baptism, of course, includes a symbolism of dying and rising, and as celebrated in the patristic period, certainly had many of the elements of ordeal and instruction we associate with initiation rites in general. However, baptism is normally celebrated either as the beginning of life or as the beginning of Christian life. Confirmation often has the timing, but little of the substance, of an initiation into adulthood. In all, it would seem that the marking of life's stages is a very minor aspect of the sacraments.

On the other hand, if we examine the sacraments, we do see close correspondences with what the mystics describe as the stages of spiritual life. These 'stages' are not tied temporally to the relevant sacraments, because most people's spiritual journey is not a simple linear affair but a path with many twists, turns and backtrackings. It is better to think of the sacraments as providing a map, or some signposts, of the terrain through which the Christian travels, than to think of them as railway stations through which she travels in a fixed linear sequence; still less as the spiritual locomotive that will haul her from one station to the next!

The Greek language distinguishes two sorts of time: *kairos*, the moment, season or opportune time, and *chronos*, duration or ongoing time. In the sacraments we need to distinguish the *kairos* when they are administered from the *chronos* in which they transform life.

> Time weds the inherent duration of the sacrament to all of human life. The time of baptism is the whole life of the Christian. And all the world knows that a marriage is not just experienced in the singing and feasting, but that it lasts through days, months and years. The grace of the sacrament is not given solely at the moment when one finds oneself in front of the priest. It is the power of the Spirit, ceaselessly offered, ceaselessly to be accepted. (Béguerie and Duchesneau, 1980, p. 36)

Here 'time' is used in the sense of *chronos*, as opposed to 'moment' or *kairos*. *Kairos* implies a due season or opportune moment for any sacrament, but this does not have to coincide with the ongoing work of the Spirit.

Sacraments and Spirituality

If we adopt this approach we can see a deep connection between the three rites associated with initiation and the traditional three stages of the spiritual journey.

1 **Baptism** has clear links with *purgation*, the stage where we repent of sin and turn our lives around to begin the journey to God. It purges or cleanses us from sin and begins a new creation in us. In baptism we 'die' to self and begin to 'rise' in Christ; we are stripped naked of self to put on Christ. The geographical image of this is the wilderness – the desert into which Christ's own baptism propelled him, in the heart of which is the split rock and the flowing stream.

2 **Confirmation** links with the way of *illumination*, where the divine light begins to shine more clearly, and the Spirit steadily teaches us and trans-

figures us. As chrismation anoints the senses to see the light, hear the voice, smell the fragrance, taste the food and feel the touch of God in all things, so this stage is one of steady growth in which our whole experience of life is affirmed but subtly transfigured. The mystics visualize this in terms of steady ascent up a mountain. We gradually see more and more, but also cloud may hide both the view of the world below and the view of the peak above, and we have to go on ascending, no longer by sight but by faith.

3 **Holy communion** links with the way of *union*, the eating and drinking with God upon the mountain (Exod. 24, see p. 24). Through the cloud we learn to live by faith, hope and love alone, the very things that can bring us to union with the divine, or what the Greek fathers called *theosis*, which literally means 'godding'. Here the loneliness of the ascent in confirmation gives way to fellowship as we find God in communion with one another. Richard of St Victor describes union not as an ultimate loss of self in God, but as the point at which the self, infused in God, becomes filled with God's mission into the world, and returns down the mountainside, as Moses did, with a new grasp of God's will for the world. Likewise the eucharist ends with a *missa*, a sending out.

The other Catholic sacraments can be seen as further effective pointers on the spiritual journey:

- *Penance or reconciliation* renews the repentance and new life brought by baptism, and effects a new purging of the soul, in which we are further stripped of and delivered from idolatrous and magic notions of God and self, to be surrounded by a fuller and truer comprehension of his love. This relates to what St John of the Cross referred to as the active nights of sense and soul, where we actively work with God to destroy the idolatrous selfish attachments of our lives, to live solely for God and in God.
- *Healing* shows forth, perhaps, the 'cloud' side of illumination: the transfiguration of our souls and bodies into the likeness of Christ continuing through suffering and affliction, bringing us to wholeness, whether or not physical healing occurs. This relates to what St John called the passive night of sense and soul, where attachments and consolations are torn

away from us against our will, leaving us on the 'wayless way' of John Ruysbroeck, bewildered until we learn to repose in God alone.

- *Marriage.* The sexual and lifelong union between man and wife has from St Paul onwards been viewed as pointing to the mystery of the soul's union with God. Marriage is then a little natural eucharist in which two people become one body, passionately indwelling one another.
- *Ordination* perhaps underlines the more active, rather than passive or passionate aspect of union with God, where this union turns outward into mission and vocation. Between them marriage and ordination show forth what Matthew Fox describes as the way of creation and creativity.

Discussion

Discuss this account of the relation between sacraments and mysticism. To what part of your experience does it relate, or fail to?

Reviving the Catechumenate: Phased Initiation

Aware that the church is in a new, 'missionary' situation in which many come to faith and the need for baptism in gradual stages, rather than being 'born' into a world in which faith can be assumed, the Roman Catholic Church has looked for resources to the early catechumenate, which was designed for a similar missionary situation in a pagan world. In 1972 it set out radical new provisions as a 'Rite of Christian Initiation for Adults' (RCIA), which is in effect a series of rites interwoven with instruction, in four stages. Key to the process is the notion that the stages are not fixed in time, but proceed at a pace fixed by the individual as his own spiritual journey unfolds. The ritual engine does not drive the individual passengers, but vice versa. On the other hand, the individual is not left to his own devices, but travels a) with a companion – the sponsor, as in the old catechumenate – in b) a community of fellow travellers on the way to faith, and within c) the wider worshipping community of the church where the distinct stages are celebrated. The church members are in turn enriched by this reminder of their own stages of faith; and as we have seen, their own liturgical year, at least from Lent through to Pentecost, was originally framed for just this purpose.

Here is the process, consisting of four stages (1–4) separated by three rites (a–c):

1 **Evangelization Stage** A loose-knit programme designed to introduce and explain the Christian faith to enquirers, leading hopefully to an initial conversion and desire to become a Christian. This leads to

a *Rite of acceptance* as a catechumen (learner). The candidates are named and asked to affirm that they seek faith leading to eternal life. They are given a Gospel book, and signed with the cross on the forehead and optionally all the senses, by the priest and their sponsor.

2 **Catechumenate Stage** A time of learning, at the candidates' own pace, with optional exorcisms and blessings. When ready they move to the next, more public stage.

b *Rite of election or enrolment* At the beginning of Lent, the candidates are presented by their sponsors and affirmed by the whole congregation, after which their names are entered in the book of those to be baptized at Easter. They are dismissed before the eucharist is celebrated.

3 **Purification and Enlightenment Stage** Deepening spiritual preparation through Lent, including scrutinies or searchings of conscience, prayer, fasting and exorcism and the learning of the Lord's prayer and creed.

c *Baptism, confirmation and first communion* at the Easter Vigil.

4 **Mystagogical Stage** An ancient word meaning 'initiation into the mysteries'. The newly initiated and their sponsors reflect on and deepen their faith journey together, and explore ways of expressing it in acts of charity.

The ecumenical *Emmaus* course (2003) is based around a simplified version of the RCIA, developing the fundamental notion that mature Christians may learn best alongside newly developing ones and especially through the responsibilities of accompanying a new Christian as a sponsor. The notion of 'unpacking' sacraments and other rites into stages carefully linked into people's own life-journeys is fundamental to the avowed approach of the Church of England's new *Common Worship*. There is as yet no equivalent of the RCIA in *Common Worship*, though this seems to be planned, with rites along *Emmaus* lines.

As it stands, however, the *Common Worship* baptism is monolithic, presupposing complete faith, rather than just the beginnings. There is at present a great tension between the pastoral and spiritual, staged approach just mentioned, and theological and ecumenical pressures to see baptism as a complete and total initiation.

The continuance of infant baptism as the norm also means that for many the beautiful stages of RCIA and its equivalents are not an option, since that process centres on adult baptism at Easter. It is possible pastorally to adapt it to become the provision for adult or adolescent confirmation candidates, though the confusion relating to that sacrament may then complicate the theological coherence of the RCIA. This brings us to the next issue.

Does Baptism Make a Christian?

Following the work of G. W. H. Lampe and others, noted in the previous chapter, there has been a growing consensus that baptism includes the giving of the Spirit and is a complete and unrepeatable incorporation into the church. BEM states:

> *Article B14* In God's work of salvation, the paschal mystery of Christ's death and resurrection is inseparably linked with the pentecostal gift of the Holy Spirit. Similarly, participation in Christ's death and resurrection is inseparably linked with the receiving of the Spirit. Baptism in its full meaning signifies and effects both.

Two sets of Christians might disagree. One is those Protestants for whom baptism is only a sign, and does not effect regeneration. For this group, becoming a Christian is a conscious, personal process of conversion, which baptism may express, but not effect. Some, but not all of this group will prefer to defer baptism until the faith it expresses is there in the believer. BEM responds very diplomatically:

> *Article B12* Both the baptism of believers and the baptism of infants take place in the church as the community of faith. When one who can answer for himself or herself is baptized, a personal confession of faith will be an

integral part of the baptismal service. When an infant is baptized, the personal response will be offered at a later moment in life. In both cases, the baptized person will have to grow in the understanding of faith. For those baptized upon their own confession of faith, there is always the constant requirement of a continuing growth of personal response in faith. In the case of infants, personal confession is expected later, and Christian nurture is directed to the eliciting of this confession. All baptism is rooted in and declares Christ's faithfulness unto death. It has its setting within the life and faith of the church and, through the witness of the whole church, points to the faithfulness of God, the ground of all life in faith. At every baptism the whole congregation reaffirms its faith in God and pledges itself to provide an environment of witness and service. Baptism should, therefore, always be celebrated and developed in the setting of the Christian community.

So personal faith and conversion are integral to baptism, but may be expected to come later rather than being already present in the individual. In any case they are already present in the Christian community. Here the burden of faith is shifted from the godparents to the community as a whole, a shift reflected in many but not all modern rites. Thus in *Common Worship* the congregation may join the parents and godparents in signing the candidates with the cross, and in the profession of faith.

The other group dissenting from BEM is those who would see chrismation (or confirmation) and first communion as integral to Christian initiation, along with baptism. We have seen that the patristic rites always construe these as parts of one process of initiation. Eastern theology had a very clear and beautiful teaching about the distinct meaning of chrismation. So Pseudo-Macarius writes (Homilies, H, 16.13 and 17.1, in 1992),

Do you not realize or understand your own nobility? Each of those who have been anointed with the heavenly chrism becomes a Christ by grace, so that all are kings and prophets of the heavenly mysteries.

But a western theologian could write in similar vein:

In Old Testament times only kings and priests received a mystical anointing. But after our Lord, the true king and eternal priest, had been anointed by God the heavenly Father with this mystical unction, it was no longer only kings and priests but the whole church that was consecrated with the anointing of chrism, because every person in the church is a member of the eternal King and Priest. Because we are a royal and priestly nation, we are anointed after the washing of baptism, that we may be bearers of the name of Christ. (Alcuin, *On the Divine Office*, 16–17)

BEM diplomatically acknowledges that 'Christians differ in their understanding as to where the sign of the gift of the Spirit is to be found', and refers concisely to the Eastern theology in its commentary on Article B14:

> Within some traditions it is explained that as baptism conforms us to Christ crucified, buried and risen, so through chrismation Christians receive the gift of the pentecostal Spirit from the anointed Son.

Discussion

Do you think the arguments that baptism makes one a Christian are convincing?

Who Should Be Baptized?

The churches answer this question in four different ways.

1 Those who ask and their children. This was the mainstream view for much of Christian history. It is enshrined in the Anglican Book of Common Prayer and canon law that the priest should not delay to baptize the children of those who ask. Lurking behind this is often the fear that because of original sin, the unbaptized will not enter heaven.
2 Those who are prepared to commit themselves and their children to learning more about the Christian faith.
3 Christian believers and their children.
4 Christian believers only. The Baptist and Anabaptist approach.

The answer given will largely depend on how we answer the previous question – on whether baptism makes a Christian. If baptism makes one a complete Christian, initiates one into the royal priesthood and commits one to Christian discipleship and apostleship, it is nonsense indiscriminately to create little 'apostles' who are likely to grow up knowing very little indeed of the Christian faith! But if baptism is just the beginning of a long journey into faith, one will be more inclined to accept tiny mustard seeds of faith. So options 2) or 3) seem to be implied by the BEM statement Article B12 above, with its high understanding of baptism as complete initiation. And many churches are moving towards this view, though there is great variation between congregations.

In the modern context, then, is there anything to be said for option 1)? In *Skandala*[1] I argue for the baptism of infants:

When we baptize children ... we are not forcing on them a repentance they cannot need or understand. Nor are we forcing them to join a separate new community of Christians, without possibly being able to understand the choice they are making. If either of these meanings – repentance, or joining the church – were primary to baptism, then those who argue that infant baptism is an aberration would be right. But if the baptism of Christ (especially as it stands in Mark) is our model, then baptism is our *genesis*, our birth as children of God by the Spirit, in Christ, from the abyss. It is then utterly appropriate at the beginning of life. In baptism we mark our children for the life that can only come about through death with Christ, through the kind of birthing sacrifice a mother understands. The font is the womb that can only be reached through the tomb.

If this is so, then repentance and belonging to Christ are both part of the meaning of baptism, but not the core. Repentance is part, because it is the way later in life we will reawaken the re-birthing process, dying to sin and being born anew to the life and love of Christ. The baby does not understand sin and repentance, but presumably it remembers far more vividly than we – in its being if not its mind – the original birth, and what it is to be born through pain and trauma into the world of light. Again, belonging to Christ and his church is part of the meaning of baptism, because it is in Christ, not alone, we die and live again. A death without him is desolate and unredeeming. We need him, and his church, so that safely the child may grow to risk this process of dying and being reborn, which is inevitable in life. Nevertheless Christ shows the way for all humanity. He does not mark out a special community of the baptized with a separate identity from the rest of the world.

Here we look to the suggestion made in Chapter 6 above, that in his baptism, Christ identified with sinful human life and took it into his own divine life. In baptism today the child is therefore likewise identified with that universal human story of brokenness and sin, in sure knowledge that Christ has already transformed that life by the baptismal fire of his divinity, and in hope that the child will in time personally make his story her own. The child now belongs to the church because the church is the way we belong fully to the humanity God in Christ has made God's own. After Christ's baptism we see how 'God the Holy Spirit "drives" Jesus the Word into the wilderness of human lostness, precisely so that even there God may be encountered' (McIntosh, 1998, p. 157). For the same purpose, we must believe, the Spirit now drives the church of the baptized into the heart of humanity.

If this is the case, then we need additional rites to mark that personal Spirit-led becoming; and perhaps this is what confirmation, chrismation or first communion are for. But we affirm in baptism that the world is already ultimately church, because its sacramental showing of the divine has already been given back to it through Christ's incarnation, baptism, death and resurrection. Of course, that ultimate identity has yet to be worked out historically in people's conscious lives. That historical outworking of redemption already accomplished in Christ is the ongoing work of the Spirit. Maybe a separate sacrament, or maybe a phased set of pastoral rites, is appropriate to signpost and enable that work. But to compress all that into a single sacrament of baptism may be less valid theologically, and less helpful pastorally and spiritually, than BEM and others would have us believe.

Discussion

Who should we baptize?

Who Do Sacraments Belong To? Baptism and Society

We have seen how baptism changed in response to changing relations to society. From an early openness and informality, it turned under persecution to the rigours of the catechumenate. In the period of Christendom, when newborn children could be assumed to be little Christians, infant baptism became the norm. So what is the appropriate way to administer baptism now, as we move to a certainly post-Christendom, and debatably post-Christian age?

At the heart of these issues about baptism are wider issues for the church and its sacraments in a changing world: Who are they *for*? Typically congregations can feel that their sacraments are being stolen from them by a couple who bring children to church for baptism without any intention of church commitment, while the couple feel that baptism belongs to their child by right, and resent the church's attempts to appropriate the rite exclusively for its committed members.

The answer to the question of who sacraments are for will depend on how the church sees its relation to surrounding culture. Here the well-known typology of the American theologian Richard Niebuhr (1975) may be useful. He detailed five ways in which Christ and his kingdom can relate to human culture, and we shall see how they imply different approaches to the sacraments.

1 **Christ against culture** This is a natural option for the church in periods of persecution, whether by a surrounding pagan culture as in the early church or parts of the developing world, or by a surrounding mainstream church culture, as with the sects of the radical reformation (for sadly, Christians have often been persecuted more by fellow Christians than by others, at least until the twentieth century). On this understanding, Christian life and ethics are radically opposed to those of society and Christians must seek to keep their ethic pure and undiluted, and convert as many as possible to it. Sacraments here will be weapons in the armoury of the church's struggle against the world, with a strong emphasis on conversion and

submission to Christ in baptism, and the gathering of God's holy people in holy communion. In both cases access to the sacraments will probably be limited to the faithful. In terms of our three dimensions the emphasis will be on the transformation of *individual life.*

2 **Christ of culture** The classic 'liberal Protestant' view which Niebuhr himself was questioning. Christ and his kingdom represent simply human culture and values at their best. The sacraments belong to the world, where the church simply serves to administer them. So the sacraments celebrate the world. Baptism serves to celebrate birth, with little emphasis on promises; the eucharist celebrates and consecrates life and community; marriage celebrates love; and so forth. The emphasis is on the *blessing of ordinary matter.*

3 **Christ above culture** This option allows the validity of human culture and accepts institutions running according to a 'natural law' ethic, but sets above this a higher Christian ethic based on divine law revealed through Christ. This represents the view of Thomas Aquinas and classical Catholicism. Here the sacraments provide a glimpse of the heavenly kingdom above, which confirms the sacramental, hierarchical order of the world as an ascent to the divine. Baptism on this view is a natural first stage of the soul's ascent, bringing the child simultaneously into the order of the world and the 'supernatural' of the church. The eucharist becomes a sacrifice, a sacred act that intercedes for and restores the world. The emphasis is on participation through earthly society in the heavenly or *sacred* one above, and on the *past traditions* through which the sacred has been passed down.

4 **Christ the transformer of culture** Here Christians are called to transform society according to kingdom values. Society is affirmed as the focus of the church's activity, but also criticized in the light of the radically different values of the kingdom, so that the church is very aware of both the need to understand the world as it is, and of its calling to represent something distinct. The church of the catechumenate period seems to represent such a position, with its combination of readiness to explain Christ to surrounding culture in its own terms, and rigour regarding membership; but so, in a different way, does liberation theology and its base communities, working from local need to programmes of transformation. Here

sacraments are effective signs of the kingdom. In baptism the catechu-menate approach fits this understanding well in the way it leads carefully from wherever people find themselves to the awesome totality of commit-ment. In all the sacraments, the focus will be directed to transformation of individual and society into the *coming kingdom of God*.

5 **Christ and culture in paradox** Here, as in 1, an extreme tension exists between the fallen world and a redeemed Christian ethos, but Christians cannot simply opt out of the former into the latter. Rather, they share in the world's fallen state and are called to establish the values of God's kingdom within the limits set by the fall. This seems to be Niebuhr's ideal view. It takes something from traditional Augustinianism and Niebuhr's own Lutheranism, with their bare juxtaposition of the two cities or king-doms and their strong emphasis on original sin. The sacraments, on such a view, might have a strong but ambiguous *social* dimension. They would belong neither to the church nor to society as such, but would celebrate membership of a redeemed world on the one hand, and a fallible church on the other. Baptism and preparation for it, for example, might be a mat-ter for creative negotiation and discovery between parents and minister, rather than for preconceived policies, whether rigorist or open; though Niebuhr himself does not argue for this.

To the above list we might add a possibility which to Niebuhr in his Ameri-can context may not have been so apparent as it is to those in more secular-ized Western Europe:

Christ the subculture Here Christians abandon relations with the main cul-ture, if indeed in a postmodern world there is any longer any 'main culture' rather than a plurality of subcultures. The church accepts being one co-existing culture among many, and develops its own life according to its own lights. If members of 'other' cultures find baptism relevant to their needs, it can only be by virtue of a confusion, since baptism, it will be argued, makes sense only in the sacramental culture of the church. The task of the church is then to develop, enrich and perhaps diversify its own culture in a way that maximizes its attractiveness to others, providing excellent opportunities for people who feel the attraction to negotiate the difficult transition from their previous culture to 'the Christian alternative'. Such a rationale may lie behind many arguments for rigorous baptism policy, and in a society where it is increasingly hard to discern a mainstream culture to relate to in any of Niebuhr's ways, it may be seen by many as the most reasonable option to take. However, others will argue that it is too introverted in the way it abandons hope of meaningful engagement in any of Niebuhr's ways.

Discussion

Where, if anywhere, would you place your views in this scheme, and how would this work out in how you think the sacraments should be celebrated?

Case Studies

This chapter has looked at many kinds of theological options, but we need to earth the discussion by relating it to pastoral practice. So in the following, imagine you are the priest or minister of the church, a) say what you would like to be able to do, and b) say what understanding of sacraments, church and society underlies your decision. You may also wish to say which policies of your own denomination would help or hinder your response.

This could be done in groups, each focusing on one question in detail then reporting back. Or if appropriate, fieldwork could be included, gleaning through interviews with ministers, church members and if possible recipients what policies apply a) in their denomination and b) specifically in their local church, and c) if possible, what the reasoning behind these policies is in terms of church, sacraments and society.

1 Mary, a girl of six who has been attending your church and Sunday school for two years says, out of the blue, she would like to be christened. Mary's parents do not come to church (and she says they are unlikely to come to the christening) but she comes to church with her friends. Last week the Sunday school teacher talked about baptism, and it emerged that all her friends were baptized but she was not.

2 An unmarried couple, Sean and Sarah, who never attend church, come to you asking you to christen their new baby boy. They are specially anxious to have him 'done' soon because next month he has to have an operation which he may not survive. They have asked at their local church but the minister refuses to do it unless they attend a six-month preparation course first. So they have come to your church, which is the one where Sarah was christened. Sean has never been christened and is very sceptical about Christian faith, though Sarah thinks there may be something in it.

3 Bill, a widower, says he would like to receive holy communion. He is quite ill and housebound and cannot attend church, and has never been baptized. He attended Sunday school as a child where he developed, for a time, a simple faith. That died out as he grew up and he only went occasionally to church, mainly to please his wife, Sue, who had a strong faith. But now he feels a desire to be close to Jesus through the sacrament, and wants to make sure that when he dies he can go to heaven and be with Sue.

4 The Sunday School teachers have been asking for permission for the children to be allowed to receive communion before confirmation, and the matter is being discussed on your church council. Which way will you argue?

Dimensions of Baptism

Figure 4 displays a summary of what we have learnt, plus some points that are clarified at particular points in the book. (The 'kingdom value' was discussed in Chapter 5 'From the Mystery to the Mysteries', and 'Spirituality' earlier in this chapter on p. 104. Meanwhile the 'church' awaits discussion in Chapter 10, 'Sacraments and the Making of the Church', and 'Cosmos' at Chapter 11, 'Sacraments and the whole living Organism'.)

Baptism is rooted in our organic need for cleansing and renewal; our need both to live with chaos and to separate ourselves from it. As God created the world through breathing his Spirit on the watery chaos, and then separated light from dark in creation, so in our baptism Christ comes to us through his baptism of death and resurrection, whereby we are reborn, and belong to a

Figure 4. Dimensions of Baptism.

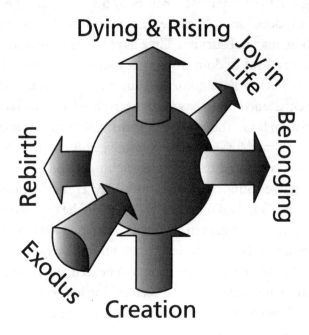

'christened' humanity through the church. In baptism we commit ourselves and our dependants to the pains and joys of the exodus journey into this freedom. We pass through the seas of Christ's death, and are reborn to the joy of eternal life.

Dimensions of Confirmation

Figure 5 sums these up. The chrism roots the sacrament in the richness of sense experience, through which all learning comes. So Christ comes in this sacrament as the teacher, encouraging us, leading us on the path of ever greater vision, deeper hearing, sweeter sensing, till we are transfigured to reflect his light as another Christ, an anointed king or queen, a devoted priest, equipped by the Spirit for the daunting responsibilities of apostleship. If these gifts are implicit in baptism, here they become explicit and conscious.

Figure 5. Dimensions of Confirmation.

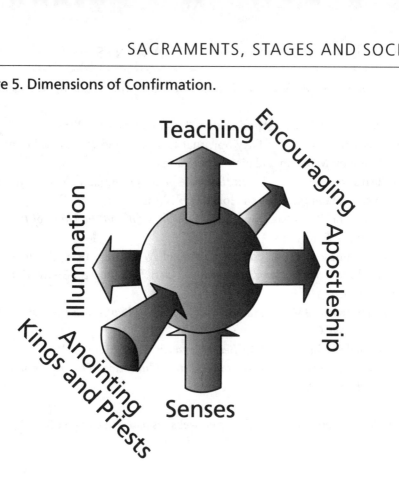

Further Reading

John Baillie, 1964, *Baptism and Conversion*, Oxford: Oxford University Press, 1964.

P. Béguerie and C. Duchesneau, 1980, *How to Understand the Sacraments*, London: SCM Press.

Colin Buchanan, 1993, *Infant Baptism and the Gospel: The Church of England's dilemma*, London: Darton, Longman and Todd.

Raymond Burnish, 1985, *The Meaning of Baptism: A comparison of the teaching and practice of the fourth century with the present day*. London: SPCK.

Church House Publishing, 1995, *On the Way: Towards an integrated approach to Christian initiation*, London: Church House Publishing.

Church House Publishing, 2003, *Emmaus: The Way of faith*, London: Church House Publishing, vol. 1: *Nurture*.

Mark Dalby, 1989, *Open Baptism*, London: SPCK.

Maxwell E. Johnson (ed.), 1995, *Living Water, Sealing Spirit: Readings on Christian initiation*, Collegeville, Minnesota: The Liturgical Press.

Mark McIntosh, 1998, *Mystical Theology*, Oxford and Malden, Massachusetts: Blackwell.

Richard Niebuhr, 1975, *Christ and Culture*, London: HarperCollins.

Pseudo-Macarius, 1992, The Fifty Spiritual Homilies and the Great Letter, trans. G. A. Maloney, Mahwah and New York: Paulist Press.

Martin Reardon, 1991, *Christian Initiation: A policy for the Church of England; a discussion paper*, London: Church House Publishing.

Michael Root and Risto Saarine (eds), 1998, *Baptism and the Unity of the Church*, Grand Rapids: Eerdmans.

David M. Thompson, et al., edited by Donald A. Withey, 1988, *Adult Initiation: Papers delivered at the Conference of the Society for Liturgical Study*, Cambridge: Grove Books.

Max Thurian (ed.), 1983, *Ecumenical Perspectives on Baptism, Eucharist and Ministry*, Geneva: WCC.

World Council of Churches, 1999, *Becoming a Christian*, Geneva: WCC.

Edward Yarnold, 1994, *The Awe-Inspiring Rites of Initiation: The origins of the RCIA*, Edinburgh: T & T Clark.

See also the ecumenical publications and websites listed in Chapter 5.

Part 4

Celebrating Church: Holy Communion

8

Evolution of the Eucharist

In the previous part we discussed the sacraments of Christian becoming, and saw that the way the church marks the process of becoming Christian through symbols and sacraments also defines different ways in which the church 'comes to be' in relation to a changing world. We now turn to the central sacrament whereby the church constitutes its very being by 'celebrating' the Trinity – giving thanks to the Father through and for the presence of Christ realized by the transfiguring power of the Spirit in its midst.

Though sometimes theologians have considered this sacrament in isolation, we shall glean a better understanding if we consider it in its liturgical context, which is the act of worship that goes by various names (see later), of which the most ecumenically widespread is the eucharist. In this chapter we will be looking at the origins and development of the eucharist, as the setting within which the specific sacrament called holy communion can alone be understood.

Natural Symbols

Like baptism, the eucharist uses natural symbols that have widespread meaning for humankind, and grafts the special Christian meanings onto this base, for example:

- *The Meal* To eat together is to share the means to life, a profound symbol probably since cave-people first shared meat around the campfire. Many festive occasions – birthdays, Christmas, Passover – culminate in a shared meal. To share table fellowship is a profound act of trust and solidarity, appropriate to family and friends and to those one wishes to make peace with or collaborate with. Exclusion from a meal is a natural sign of disapproval, as when parents tell their children to go to bed without supper.

- *Sacrifice* It is natural to wish to share meals with the gods in whom one believes. All meals carry an element of sacrifice in that life has to be killed and crushed in order to be devoured. It is natural to offer the whole meal in thanksgiving to God or the gods who provide the food, as many do in saying grace. To set aside part of the meal as an offering to the gods or to the spirit of the animals that have been harmed by killing and devouring is a widespread courtesy. In time sacrifice acquired its own systems and rites. It did not always involve the shedding of blood; witness Hindu *puja*, and the Greco-Roman libation in which a cup of wine was offered to the gods. Nor did it always involve the eating of food; witness the holocaust ('whole burnt offering'), offered entirely to God. Often, of course, sacrifice could become an obsessive and all-demanding attempt to appease angry deities, awaken lazy ones, or feed voracious ones, as in the terrible human sacrifices of the Aztecs. But the roots of sacrifice in mealtime conviviality are clear.

- *Bread* is the ordinary, staple diet of many peoples, including our own. Breaking bread at a meal significantly does not involve the taking of life, but the preparing of the bread involves a fourfold dying: one natural, the sowing, whereby seed falls to the ground, 'dies' and rises as wheat; and three involving the sacrifice of human labour: the harvesting, the grinding of the grain to make flour, and the baking of dough to make the bread.

- *Wine* is the staple drink in the Mediterranean, fermentation being a natural way of preserving the juice of the grape and rendering it, through the alcohol, safe from infection. Obviously wine also connotes a special conviviality at a meal, bringing an increased enjoyment of life, shared together, and pure, good wine was not cheap in Jesus' time, probably beyond the reach of the poor. As with bread, there is no sacrifice in drinking wine, but a sacrificial process of pruning, harvesting, crushing and fermenting precedes the drinking. The old English ballad of Sir John Barleycorn testifies to a folk-awareness of the many 'deaths' necessary in the similar process of making ale from barley, describing him being buried, scythed down, bound on carts, winnowed with sticks, crushed between mill-stones, mashed and fermented. In addition, being the colour of blood, red wine tends to suggest a sacrificial sharing of life together.

Jewish Antecedents

Bread and wine both figure in Jewish worship and festival. The 'bread of the presence' was kept in the temple, commemorating the manna by which the Jews were fed in the wilderness. As noted, wine was drunk at Passover, the feast of liberation, while other texts associate wine with the promised messianic reign:

> On this mountain the Lord of hosts will make for all peoples
> a feast of rich food, a feast of well-aged wines,
> of rich food filled with marrow, of well-aged wines strained clear.
> And he will destroy on this mountain
> the shroud that is cast over all peoples,
> the sheet that is spread over all nations;
> he will swallow up death for ever. (Isaiah 25.6–8a)

However, some texts (like Ps. 75.8) associate wine with intoxication as a punishment, while others even more vividly associate the winepress with punishment through bloodshed. Isaiah 63.1–6 asks God or his prophet why his robes are stained red, and he replies, in terms that some apply to the pouring out of God's wrath in the shedding of Christ's blood on the cross:

> I have trodden the wine press alone,
> and from the peoples no one was with me;
> I trod them in my anger
> and trampled them in my wrath;
> their juice spattered on my garments,
> and stained all my robes.

Fellowship meals (*charubah*) were frequently shared by teachers and disciples in Israel. Special delicacies would be shared, often with symbolic meanings. Then there would be ablutions and the main meal, including prayers of blessing over the food and various cups of wine, then further ablutions and a final psalm. The prayer (*birkath* or *berakah*) would bless the meal by way of blessing God for it, as in the blessing of bread: 'Blessed are you, Lord God of the universe, for you bring forth bread from the earth'. It is quite easy to see the last supper as one such meal, and to trace the eucharistic (thanksgiving) prayer back to such Jewish prayers of blessing.

Finally, the great Jewish feasts discussed in Chapter 2 (p. 21) carried meanings that Christians, later, would draw into the eucharist:

- *Passover* The synoptic Gospels describe Jesus' last supper as a Passover meal, whereas John sees it as a fellowship meal celebrated on the eve of Passover. The latter has been argued to be more likely, since the Jewish priests would not have wanted to busy themselves organizing the crucifixion in the sacred time following the Passover sacrifice. But in any event the supper and crucifixion took place in the broad context of a Passover festival, and Passover themes of hope of liberty from 'Egypt' and the coming of the messianic reign are central to the Christian eucharist. Jesus is identified in Paul as the sacrificed Passover lamb that brings freedom (1 Cor. 5.7–8).
- *Covenant* Jesus relates the wine to the blood of the covenant (see Table 3). In Paul this covenant denotes a new relation to God based not on law and obedience but on forgiveness and response. The wine thus points three ways: to the bull's blood of the old covenant, the blood shed on the cross, and the hope for a new peaceable covenant of wine and kingdom conviviality between God and humankind.
- *Day of Atonement* There is little reference in the last supper to the scapegoat driven into the wilderness, but suffering servant imagery, which is based on the goat that bears the penalty of others' sins, was applied in the New Testament to Jesus' suffering and death, not least in the curious description attributed to John the Baptist, of Jesus as 'the Lamb of God who takes away the sin of the world' (John 1.29). Here the Passover lamb and the atonement goat are fused into one.

- *Pentecost* Paul calls Jesus the 'first-fruits' of the resurrection (1 Cor. 15.20, 23), relating him to the offering made at Pentecost. His supper is seen as looking forward to the establishment of the kingdom, the beginning of the end-time, hence his words about not drinking wine till the kingdom comes (see Table 3 below).

The Last Supper

In the New Testament, obviously the narratives of the last supper are crucial to an understanding of the eucharist. Let's look at them more closely.

Exercise

Look at the relevant texts, set out in Table 3, and mark
- What is *common* to all?
- What are *distinctive* to particular Gospels?
- If you had to divide the accounts into *two types*, how would you do it?
- Why are only three Gospels listed?

Paul was relating a tradition 'received from the Lord' about 20 or 30 years after Jesus' death, and Luke follows him quite closely in describing the wine as the 'covenant in my blood', drunk after supper; though Luke includes also the words about the kingdom (in a different place from the other two Gospels). Those two relate the words over the cup in a simpler, barer form, and place both bread and cup within the meal.

   One line of scholarly argument ascribes these words to Christian assimilation of the Greek mystery cults, projected back onto Jesus' words and actions that he, as a Jew abhorring the thought of drinking blood, could not have intended. However, in their free, innovative use of liturgy and their startling, almost offensive challenge, the words seem to bear the mark of Jesus, and the multiple attestation, in only slightly different forms, suggests they derive from him. What he intended by them is, of course, a matter of fierce controversy, to which we shall turn in the next chapter.

Table 3. Last Supper Narratives.

	Matthew 26.26–29	Mark 14.22–25	Luke 22.15–21	1 Cor. 11.23–25
Before			He said to them, 'I have eagerly desired to eat this Passover with you before I suffer; for I tell you, I will not eat it until it is fulfilled in the kingdom of God.' Then he took a cup, and after giving thanks he said, 'Take this and divide it among yourselves; for I tell you that from now on I will not drink of the fruit of the vine until the kingdom of God comes.'	For I received from the Lord what I also handed on to you, that the Lord Jesus on the night when he was betrayed.
The bread	While they were eating, Jesus took a loaf of bread, and after blessing it he broke it, gave it to the disciples, and said, 'Take, eat; this is my body.'	While they were eating, he took a loaf of bread, and after blessing it he broke it, gave it to them, and said, 'Take; this is my body.'	Then he took a loaf of bread, and when he had given thanks, he broke it and gave it to them, saying, 'This is my body, which is given for you. Do this in remembrance of me.'	took a loaf of bread, and when he had given thanks, he broke it and said, 'This is my body that is for you. Do this in remembrance of me.'

| The cup | Then he took a cup, and after giving thanks he gave it to them, saying, 'Drink from it, all of you; for this is my blood of the covenant, which is poured out for many for the forgiveness of sins. | Then he took a cup, and after giving thanks he gave it to them, and all of them drank from it. He said to them, 'This is my blood of the covenant, which is poured out for many. | And he did the same with the cup after supper, saying, 'This cup that is poured out for you is the new covenant in my blood. | In the same way he took the cup also, after supper, saying, 'This cup is the new covenant in my blood. Do this, as often as you drink it, in remembrance of me. |
| After | I tell you, I will never again drink of this fruit of the vine until that day when I drink it new with you in my Father's kingdom.' | Truly I tell you, I will never again drink of the fruit of the vine until that day when I drink it new in the kingdom of God.' | But see, the one who betrays me is with me, and his hand is on the table.' | For as often as you eat this bread and drink the cup, you proclaim the Lord's death until he comes.' |

William Vanstone (2004) has noted that the word which Paul uses for 'tradition' and 'passing on' – *paradosis* – is the same as is used for 'betrayal' of Judas; the literal meaning is 'hand over' or 'hand on'. The concept appears twice in 1 Corinthians 11.23, which could thus be translated, 'For I took over (*paralabo*, a related term) from the Lord what I also handed over to you, that the Lord Jesus on the night when he was handed over . . .' Jesus therefore 'hands over' a 'handing over' (tradition) at the very time in which he is being personally 'handed over' (betrayed) to death. All the Gospels link the giving of the bread and wine with the betrayal, and this is particularly striking in Luke's account, above. The eucharist represents a handing over of the body and the life of Jesus, which is at once faithful tradition and and in some sense a betrayal.

Other Meals in the Gospels

The route from the last supper to the eucharist as we know it is not straightforward, and not all scholars would trace a single clear route. Paul Bradshaw (2004), for example, traces a variety of meals in early Christianity, involving bread, wine and water in various combinations, which he traces to a variety of roots in the different meals of Jesus. These include:

- *Jesus' open table fellowship* Jesus was known for having a good time with tax-collectors, prostitutes and other outcasts. This would have been taken as a sign that in his view they were reconciled and welcomed into God's kingdom; a view that more conventional authorities could not accept. For John Crossan (1992) this 'open commensality' was highly unusual at the time and central to Jesus' message.
- *The feedings* of the 5,000 men and the 4,000 men with five loaves and two fish, described in all four Gospels. As well as showing miraculous powers, these probably point forward to Isaiah's messianic feast on the mountain (quoted above). The fish was an early symbol of Christ, which may at some stage have been used in sacramental meals. The disciples were fishermen called to be 'fishers of people' (Mark 1.17; Matt. 4.19), and the risen Christ eats fish with them in Luke 24.42 and John 21.13.

- *The Emmaus road*, a resurrection story appearing only in Luke (24.13–35). Having walked unrecognized with two otherwise unknown disciples, and expounded the word of scripture to them, Jesus is invited by them to stay the night. They recognize him 'in the breaking of bread', but at once he disappears. Some see here an allegory for the service of word (the expounding of scripture) and sacrament ('breaking of bread' being probably an early name for the eucharist).

One current controversy is whether the eucharist should be an 'open table' for all to share, or restricted to the faithful or the fully initiated. We note that the last supper and the Emmaus meal were shared with a few disciples. The open fellowship and the feedings of the crowds, on the other hand, were clearly shared indiscriminately with the *ochloi* (masses, mob, rabble). One factor in the debate, then, will be from which of these events one derives the eucharist.

Discussion

Discuss arguments for and against the 'open table'.

The Early Christian Agapé

Paul gives us the first knowledge of early Christian worship, indirectly, in 1 Corinthians, where he urges Christians to be more generous in sharing their food in their *agapés* or love festivals. Not to do so dishonours the body of Christ, he argues, and brings condemnation. He relates the last supper, as quoted above, then says,

> Whoever, therefore, eats the bread or drinks the cup of the Lord in an unworthy manner will be answerable for the body and blood of the Lord. Examine yourselves, and only then eat of the bread and drink of the cup. For all who eat and drink without discerning the body, eat and drink judgment against themselves. (1 Cor. 11.23–29)

Earlier (1 Cor. 10.16) Paul has spoken of the sharing of the bread as a *koinonia* (sharing, communion, partaking) in the body of Christ, and the sharing of the cup as a *koinonia* in his blood; the Christians are the one body of Christ as they share the one bread

Clearly this early Christian *agapé* consisted of a special meal during which bread was broken and wine shared. But does Paul mean:

- The sharing in bread is the sharing of the body of Christ in the sense of 'church', so the 'body' the reckless fail to discern is the church community; or
- The sharing in bread and wine is a sacramental sharing in the body and blood of Christ. This is what constitutes the church as body of Christ; so it is this sacramental 'body' that needs to be discerned.

This is probably a distinction Paul would not make, and indeed was not generally made until the Middle Ages. Until then 'mystical body' meant primarily the sacramental body, but also the church as body of Christ. So the above two statements form an interdependent whole: the church is church because it shares in Christ sacramentally, but the sharing of bread and wine is sacramental because it is the church's sharing. The church makes the sacrament as the sacrament makes the church.

This is not a vicious circle. Generally speaking the things we make, do and say make us the people we are even as we make them what they are; and the sacraments are no exception.

Signs of the Incarnate One, and the Heavenly Worship

Some late writings in the New Testament are also critical for understanding the eucharist.

The Gospel of John was notably absent from Table 3. John recounts the last supper without reference to the words and actions of Jesus with the bread and wine. Instead, Jesus washes the disciples' feet, an action described in no other place in the New Testament. However, we noted in Chapter 3 how in this Gospel, after the sign of the feeding of the 5,000, Jesus gives a discourse on himself as the bread of life, and on the need to eat his flesh and drink his blood. Some argue for a tradition in which the Christian love feast is based on these feedings rather than the last supper, Jesus being shown forth in bread and fish. However, the flesh and blood referred to in the discourse after the sign suggest a bread and wine, not bread and fish, tradition.

Again, some Protestants suggest that the feeding on flesh and blood denotes the need to feed on God's Word, and the omission of the bread and wine sayings at the last supper suggests that John was avoiding sacramentalism. On the other hand, the 'flesh' which Jesus' followers are invited to eat recollects the 'Word made flesh' at the beginning of the Gospel, suggesting that we need to commune with the Word bodily, not just as Word. In Chapter 3 I argued that this Gospel presents Jesus as the primal sacrament in which the cosmos becomes sign-full. If it disregards (while presupposing) particular sacraments, it is because it is the most sacramental of all the Gospels.

The Letter to the Hebrews We noted, again in Chapter 3, how Christ is here presented as both fulfilling and undermining the Jewish sacrificial system. Through the cross, Christ the high priest enters the holy of holies with his offering of himself, so taking us all to a place of free, unmediated access to the divine. As we shall see, Catholics see this as supporting sacrificial language about the eucharist, while Protestants generally criticize such language on the basis of this letter.

Finally, *Revelation*, as there noted, relates the worship of heaven in terms of the adoration of Christ the Lamb. In the Authorized version of the Bible the Lamb is slain from eternity:

All that dwell upon the earth shall worship him, whose names are not written in the book of life of the Lamb slain from the foundation of the world. (Rev. 13.8)

This passage has been used to argue that from early times Christians saw the sacrifice of Christ as having an eternal, as well as a 'once for all' historical dimension, and that in the eucharist we participate in this eternity and are mystically present at the sacrifice of the Lamb. However, the passage can be translated, as in the NRSV:

> All the inhabitants of the earth will worship it, everyone whose name has not been written from the foundation of the world in the book of life of the Lamb that was slaughtered.

Now if the names were written in the book of the slaughtered Lamb before time began, that sacrifice is at least eternally ordained, and the worship of heaven eternally goes on centring on this eternally ordained sacrifice that occurred once in time. So Revelation emphasizes the cross as having a fore-ordained and doxological (glorifying) dimension of paschal sacrifice, creating a liberating path through the dangerous seas of sin and death into the promised New Jerusalem, which remains open for ever.

So both Hebrews and Revelation see the cross as a sacrifice powerful for all time, but where Hebrews has the scapegoat and the temple in mind, revelation has the Lamb and the exodus. Both ideas are crucial to the development of the eucharist.

From Agapé to Eucharist

So far all the possible prototypes of the eucharist refer to a meal, with or without the sharing of bread and wine. Likewise the *Didaché*, a very early worship manual, describes an *agapé* or love-meal with blessing over the wine and another over the cup, a meal and a final blessing. The *berakah* over the bread, which, interestingly follows that over the cup, has a beautiful analogy:

> We give thanks to you, our Father, for the life and knowledge which you made known to us through your child Jesus; glory to you for evermore. As this broken bread was scattered over the mountains and when brought together became one, so let your church be brought together from the ends of the earth into your kingdom; for yours are the glory and the power through Jesus Christ for evermore.

The text has some very Jewish imagery, like Christ as 'Vine of David'. Some argue the text must therefore come from the late 40s, before the expulsion of the Christians from the synagogue. If so, it is one of the earliest Christian texts we have; but most scholars would date it later. It seems to develop from the last supper precisely those strands – the full meal, the Jewish blessing prayers and their imagery, the anticipation of the coming kingdom – that dropped out in later tradition, while ignoring those that later became central, such as Christ's words of institution, and the remembrance of his death and resurrection. Whether it represents a missing link or an altogether different strand of development is hard to say.

It has been suggested, first of all by Gregory Dix, that this early feast developed into the eucharist as we know it by two processes:

- The expulsion of the Christians from the synagogue, c. AD 49, creating the need for the love-feast to be a whole act of worship. The Scripture readings, preaching and prayers, which were the staple diet of the synagogue, began to form the first half of the service, known to us as the 'Ministry of the Word'.
- The dropping out of the meal as a whole, to leave precisely those parts of the meal to which Christ had given special meaning. In the process the seven actions of Jesus – taking, blessing, breaking and giving wine, taking, blessing and sharing bread – are compressed into the four that Dix saw as the backbone of the 'Ministry of the Sacrament' as we have it today: offering of bread and wine, consecrating through thanksgiving, breaking of bread, and communion.

Seminal as Dix's work was for the revision of the eucharist in all denominations, however, not all would agree with this linear evolution; the evidence of the *Didaché* is, we have seen, ambiguous, and may point to a much more complex picture.

At any rate, by the third century the eucharist as we know it had developed the shape that is familiar to Christians of all denominations today. The eucharist found in the *Apostolic Tradition* of Hippolytus, which many date around AD 215, follows a pattern close to the modern one in Figure 6, partly because modern rites have returned to it as a basic type that existed prior to the diversifications described next.

The Orthodox Liturgy

In the East the eucharist came to be called simply 'the divine liturgy'. For as the empire became Christianized under Constantine, it became a public (*leitos*) work, service or duty (*ergos*), carried out in the new church buildings. These were modelled not on temples but basilicas, the places of public meeting where rulers would meet their people and administer justice. So the liturgy formed the heart of a public pattern of life that strove to embrace the whole time of Sunday and the whole space of the city, with liturgies of the various hours, morning prayer, eucharist and evening prayer, running into each other and spread across several churches, connected by processions through the streets (cf. Kavanagh, 1981, pp. 57–9).

To this day an Orthodox Sunday morning at least has the feeling of ongoing worship which the people drop in and out of. For in the East the tendency was to preserve and elaborate, never to truncate. So the shape of the 'classic' liturgy remains intact, though somewhat occluded with repeated litanies of payers and elaborate symbolism. The liturgy dramatically re-presents the whole saving work of Christ. The first half of the liturgy focuses on the readings; it is introduced by the Little Entrance, where the Gospel Book is carried round the church, representing the first coming of Christ, the teacher of the Gospel. The second half is introduced by the Great Entrance, representing the second coming of Christ, when the bread and wine are likewise paraded and venerated, and solemn prayers of all the faithful are said over them. The cherubic hymn which accompanies this emphasizes the degree to which this earthly worship is seen as imaging the heavenly:

> Let us who in a mystery represent the cherubim and sing the thrice holy hymn to the life-giving Trinity, lay aside the cares of this life, that we may raise up the King of all, invisibly borne aloft by the angelic orders. Alleluia, alleluia, alleluia!

This entrance adds to this end-time or heavenly emphasis symbolism relating to Christ's journey to the cross. So the overall import is what the book of Revelation suggests, that here the eternal and ultimate sacrifice of Christ is being imaged by the body of Christ on earth. The kiss of peace then leads to the creed and then the eucharistic prayer. Leavened bread is used and people, including children, receive bread and wine mingled together on a spoon, this mingling symbolizing the risen Christ in whom body and blood are reunited. The words of invitation to communion express a wonderful theological balance between the holiness of the sacramental 'things', the holiness of the whole people of God, and the holiness of Christ, which alone accounts for the other forms of holiness:

Priest: Holy things for the holy!
People: One is holy, one is Lord, Jesus Christ!

This liturgy is celebrated on Sundays and festivals, and is always sung in entirety with incense and full ceremonial. The place of worship has been modified in two ways. The basilica is foreshortened, with a great dome enclosing a roughly circular, intimate space, while icons have proliferated and formed a screen separating off the priestly actions. Processions enter and leave the altar through doors in the screen, rather as actors did on the classical stage. The overall effect is of a space where heaven and earth meet, in which the faithful gather to converse with the saints represented in the icons and to be swept up in the drama of salvation.

The Catholic Mass

Western Catholicism tended, on the contrary, to rationalize the language and structure. A much simplified, said, daily mass was introduced. Unleavened bread was used, and the consecrated wine was reserved for the priests only. As in the East, actual communion became occasional, and normally attendance at mass focused on the adoration of the consecrated bread and wine. In any event the consecrated wine was reserved for the clergy, the people receiving only the host. This was justified on the grounds that all the 'parts' of Christ – body, blood, soul and divinity – were fully present in the consecrated wafer, but the move was criticized by Wycliffe and others well before the Reformation proper.

Whereas the liturgy of the Orthodox and Protestant churches is in the language of the people (albeit often in an archaic form), the Roman Church (until Vatican II) insisted on the use of Latin.

Architecture reflected the same tendency to make the holy distant and precious, rather than enveloping, familiar and awesome, as with the Orthodox. The old basilica was modified in a manner opposite to the Orthodox, being lengthened and divided into three distinct hierarchical spaces: the sanctuary in the east – divine space – with the altar placed against the east wall; the choir – angelic space – and the nave, ordinary space for the ordinary people. Vertical straight lines increased too, the Gothic architecture striving to lift the building to an immaterial, heavenly realm where stones seemed not to weigh down and enclose. The eucharist was less a drama than a remote presence, lifted up, longed for and adored.

After communion the rite ended rapidly with the blessing and the dismissal, 'Ite, missa est' ('Go, it is the sending'), from which the characteristic Roman Catholic term mass (Latin missa) takes its name. If in the East the emphasis was on the ascent from the world 'up' into the kingdom, the entry into the end time, in the West it was on channelling heaven sacramentally 'down' to earth to provide the supernatural energy needed for the missa, the mission of Christians in their day-to-day lives.

The Protestant Supper

The reformers attempted to restore regular communion in both bread and wine. Suspicious of 'works', they radically simplified the ritual, rooted out any hint of offering or sacrifice, and in many cases reduced the eucharistic prayers to the words of institution plus an exhortation to worthy reception. Great emphasis was rather placed on the Ministry of the Word, the Bible readings and preaching, while the words of the eucharist itself became didactic, instructing the faithful in the meaning of the service. The preferred names for the service – Lord's supper, breaking of bread, or holy communion – reflect the emphasis on personal memorial of Jesus, his cross and supper, and communion in him and one another. The eucharistic celebration became occasional, often quarterly, but surrounded by great solemnity, austerity and awe. However, just as in the East prayers for the world had proliferated throughout the liturgy, obscuring its shape and making for a corporate, cosmic expansiveness, so in most Protestant rites penitential material proliferated, making for a personal, contrite inwardness.

Architecturally, in Protestant churches and chapels space became foreshortened again, with galleries, making this a space for democratic assembly, but also, as in the East, a theatre. However it was now a theatre for the Word. Altar and lectern were reversed, with the latter becoming a high dominant pulpit close to the east wall, where the Word may be proclaimed, while the former became a communion table set in the midst of the people.

The Liturgical Movement and the Modern Eucharist

The nineteenth-century Oxford Movement tried to restore something close to the medieval mass to the Church of England, but it was only in the mid-twentieth century that a liturgical movement enabled all denominations to rediscover earlier patterns like the eucharist of Hippolytus, and the fourfold pattern argued by Dix. Thanks to Vatican II in the Catholic Church, the Anglican Parish Communion movement, and equivalent changes in the reformed churches, the eucharist has widely been restored as the central Sunday act of worship in many denominations. Despite this convergence, however, while most Protestant churches accept intercommunion (receiving communion at one another's churches), this is rejected by the Roman Catholics and Orthodox.

The eucharist, now widespread in the West, is illustrated in Figure 6 as a kind of interaction between the people and God, or world and kingdom, or between 'upward and inward' and 'downward and outward'. The figure makes it clear that the liturgy is an organic thing and our human ways of cutting it into segments are somewhat arbitrary; they are valid insofar as they help us discern the contours of the living thing. There are still variations from this shape – particularly in the position of the confession, creed and peace – but Figure 6 represents a widespread template.

Figure 6. The Shape of the Modern Eucharist.

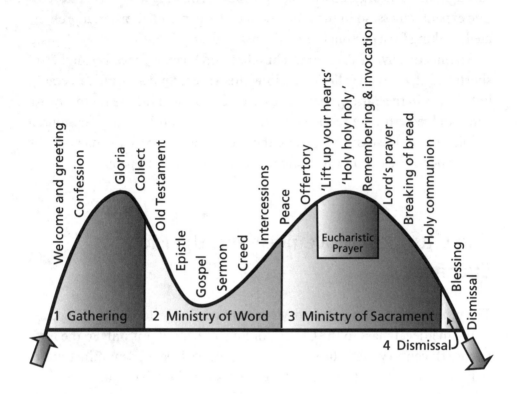

1 In the first part, the people gather and present themselves to God. They confess their sins to him and ask for his merciful love, then praise him in the first of the angelic songs, 'Glory to God in the highest'. A prayer called the 'collect' collects the people together and prepares them to hear the readings that follow.

2 Now the people receive Christ coming among his people in his word, culminating in the Gospel, often accompanied with alleluias and candles, symbols of Christ, the Light of the World. They respond with an expression of faith – the creed – and intercession for the world.

3 The people exchange a sign of peace, and lift up bread and wine and with them their whole life and their hearts. These are blessed in the great

eucharistic prayer with, at its heart, the second angelic song, the 'Holy, holy, holy', after which the 'downward' movement of Christ's Word and the Spirit's coming prevail. The Lord's prayer is said, the 'Lamb of God' is sung as bread is broken, and the consecrated bread and wine are shared by all the faithful.

4. This downward and outward movement is completed as the people are blessed and dismissed to continue their 'divine service' in the wider world.

New architecture has accompanied this new liturgical shape. Altar, lectern and font are placed with equal privilege in the centre, since in the new liturgies Word and Sacrament have equal honour. The space tends to be circular and thoroughly democratic, resembling modern architecture for parliaments. A realized kingdom, united to earth, seems to be celebrated in the liturgy, as in the Orthodox Church, but with the difference that all is open to view and there is no mystery, and little movement is necessary, since the spaces for leading Word, eucharist and Baptism are clustered at the centre. There are no hiding places for the half-committed, for all, priest included, worship facing everyone else, but away from a world that is now definitely 'outside'.

Discussion

Discuss the strengths and weaknesses of this liturgical and architectural 'shape' *vis à vis* previous alternatives.

Project

Students may try designing their own outline liturgy and/or church space and describing how these express their own understanding of the eucharist. This could be preceded by visits to churches to see a) what the liturgy and space express to a newcomer like themselves; and b) what they express to the participants.[1]

Further Reading

Archbishops' Commission on Christian Doctrine, 1972, *Thinking About the Eucharist*, London: SCM Press.

Louis Bouyer, 1968, *Eucharist: Theology and spirituality of the eucharistic prayer*, Indiana: University of Notre Dame Press.

Paul Bradshaw, 2004, *Eucharistic Origins*, London: SPCK.

Colin Buchanan, 1982, *What Did Cranmer Think He Was Doing?*, Cambridge: Grove Books.

Christopher J. Cocksworth, 1993, *Evangelical Eucharistic Thought in the Church of England*, Cambridge: Cambridge University Press.

John Dominic Crossan, 1992, *The Historical Jesus: The life of a Mediterranean Jewish peasant*, London: HarperCollins.

Dom Gregory Dix, 2001, *The Shape of the Liturgy*, London and New York: Continuum.

P. J. FitzPatrick, 1993, *In Breaking of Bread: The eucharist and ritual*, Cambridge: Cambridge University Press.

Richard Giles, 1999, *Re-Pitching the Tent: Reordering the church building for worship and mission*, Norwich: Canterbury Press.

Richard Giles, 2004, *Creating Uncommon Worship*, Norwich: Canterbury Press.

R. P. C. Hanson, 1979, *Eucharistic Offering in the Early Church*, Cambridge: Grove Books.

R. C. D. Jasper and G. J. Cuming (eds), 1975, *Prayers of the Eucharist: Early and reformed,* London: Collins.

Joachim Jeremias, 1966, *The Eucharistic Words of Jesus*, London: SCM Press.

Aidan Kavanagh, 1981, *On Liturgical Theology*, Collegeville, Minnesota: The Liturgical Press.

I. Howard Marshall, 1980, *Last Supper and Lord's Supper*, London: Paternoster.

Willy Rordorf, et al., 1976, *The Eucharist of the Early Christians*, New York: Pueblo.

Nicholas Sagovsky, 2000, *Ecumenism: Christian origins and the practice of communion*, Cambridge: Cambridge University Press.

Max Thurian, 2002, 2003, *The Eucharistic Memorial, Part 1: The Old Testament* and *Part 2: The New Testament*, London: James Clarke.

William Vanstone, 2004, *The Stature of Waiting*, London: Darton, Longman and Todd.

Tom Wright, 2002, *The Meal Jesus Gave Us: Understanding holy communion*, London: Hodder and Stoughton.

9

Theologies of the Eucharist: Presence and Sacrifice

Having charted the way the eucharist has developed in time, we turn to explore critical themes that have sometimes united, but sometimes sadly divided Christians. We explore the questions, in what sense is Christ present in the eucharist, and is the eucharist a sacrifice?

Here, we are in the realm of theologies of the eucharist. The divisions have arguably arisen as theologians have tried to apply preconceived theories of reality to the eucharist. In the next chapter we will turn to eucharistic theology – the attempt to apply the eucharist to understand and transform reality, and especially the cosmos, society and spirituality.

The Eucharistic Presence of Christ

By the mid-second century, Justin Martyr was expressing a very concrete understanding of the presence of Christ in the eucharistic bread and wine:

> We do not receive these things as common bread or common drink; but just as our Saviour Jesus Christ, being incarnate through the word of God, took flesh and blood for our salvation, so too we have been taught that the

food over which thanks have been given by the prayer of the Word who is from him, from which our flesh and blood are fed by transformation, is both the flesh and blood of that incarnate Jesus. (1997, *First Apology*, 66.2)

The Fathers generally concurred with this approach, accepting the real presence as a mystery of faith. Theologians based around Alexandria in Egypt tended to follow Justin in linking the eucharistic presence with the incarnation, while those based around Antioch in Syria thought more in terms of the presence of Jesus' saving passion and resurrection in the liturgy.

Augustine is rather typical of the Fathers in the way he balances the ecclesial mystery of the church as the body of Christ and the sacramental mystery of the body and blood:

If you wish to understand what is meant by 'the Body of Christ', listen to the apostle saying to the faithful, 'You are the Body of Christ and his members'. It is the mystery of yourselves that is laid on the Lord's table; it is the mystery of yourselves that you receive. (1994, Sermon 272)

In other words, in the offertory, we offer ourselves in the bread and wine. In the eucharistic prayer these are consecrated to become the body and blood of Christ. So what we share in communion is the mystery of ourselves transformed to become the body of Christ. When we partake of the eucharist, we do not consume him and convert him into our bodies; rather, he consumes and converts us into his body, the church.

This kind of approach remained central to Eastern understandings; after all, in the Greek terminology it was not even possible to distinguish the 'sacramental' body of Christ from the 'mystical' body of the church.

Medieval Literalism

It was not until AD 831 that people started wanting to be more precise about the sacramental body. In that year the Benedictine abbot Paschasius Radbert urged that in the mass we literally munch the flesh that Christ bore in his earthly life and repeat his sacrifice in a new 'slaughter'. He was opposed by the monk Ratramnus, who argued that the bread and wine are not physically altered but are only 'figures' and 'representations' of Christ, though bearing his reality. Later, in the eleventh century, Berengrar argued (like Calvin later) that Christ's body was in heaven so that his eucharistic presence must be spiritual, not literal. Berengrar was forced to recant and accept a more literalist view, however, employing the newly adopted Aristotelian concepts of substance and accidents, which were to inform medieval discussions.

The eucharistic bread began to be described as a host (Latin *hosta*, sacrificial victim), which the priest offered to God before breaking and sharing among the people, thus following the pattern of a Jewish or pagan sacrifice. Medieval piety meanwhile began to describe doubters having their eyes opened so that they see, in the host, not bread but bleeding flesh.

Aquinas and Transubstantiation

Aquinas argued against both Berengrar and his opponents that the bread and wine were neither literally nor purely spiritually but sacramentally the body and blood of Christ. In the by now familiar teaching, after consecration only the outward form or 'sensible accidents' of bread and wine remained. Their inward 'substance' was bread and wine no longer, being changed into Christ's body and blood. A paradoxical 'transubstantiation' had occurred.

Though vested in Aristotle's concepts, the ideas here are quite basic and not specific to any one philosophical system. 'Substance' simply denotes the answer to the question of *who or what someone or something is*, while 'accidents' refers to the things we can say about that person or thing at the moment, to describe *what they are like*. So transubstantiation is really only the notion that in the eucharist the elements stay looking like the same thing, but what they are changes.

Why was this a paradox? It is normal for things to change what they are like while staying the same thing. For instance, a tree remains a tree when its leaves change colour in the autumn. But what things are can change, as at conception (or some would say birth) when a collection of cells becomes something substantially different, namely a human being; or at death, when what was a human person becomes just a collection of cells. Here the 'substance' changes. But in such cases the 'sensible accidents' change too; otherwise we would not notice birth or death. In transubstantiation, the substantial change happens without anything noticeable happening. There is a new creation, a 'birth' of the body and blood of Christ – we could say – and a 'death' of bread and wine, without any detectable change in the accidents at all.

For Aquinas, as already discussed in Chapter 3, this is because the sacramental body is born not through a natural process of birth or death, but through the action of God in the church, which is not a natural body but a social body constituted by signs, words and beliefs. A sign made by God in the body of the church is sufficient, in Aquinas' view, to change not the appearances of bread and wine, which remain, but the essential thing they are appearances of. We will return to this after we have considered alternative, Protestant views, but note that bleeding hosts are not compatible with transubstantiation, since they involve a change in the sensible accidents.[1]

Martin Luther: Consubstantiation

Martin Luther agreed that the body and blood of Christ are truly present in the eucharist, but rejected the idea that this presence had to annihilate that of bread and wine. The elements are substantially body and bread together, and blood and wine together. (This view, described as 'consubstantiation', does not make sense in the philosophical categories with which Aquinas was working, but might to us, see later.) Moreover, after the service the elements may be treated as simply bread and wine; it is not right to adore them as Christ's body and blood outside of the eucharist. Finally, Luther followed Aquinas in believing that 'faith alone' could perceive the body and the blood in the eucharist, and receive their benefits in the soul.

Anglicanism: Real but Spiritual Partaking

The Book of Common Prayer states, in Article 28:

> The Supper of the Lord is not only a sign of the love that Christians ought to have among themselves one to another; but rather is a Sacrament of our

Redemption by Christ's death: insomuch that to such as rightly, worthily, and with faith, receive the same, the Bread which we break is a partaking of the Body of Christ; and likewise the Cup of Blessing is a partaking of the Blood of Christ.

Transubstantiation (or the change of the substance of Bread and Wine) in the Supper of the Lord, cannot be proved by holy Writ; but is repugnant to the plain words of Scripture, overthroweth the nature of a Sacrament, and hath given occasion to many superstitions.

The Body of Christ is given, taken, and eaten, in the Supper, only after an heavenly and spiritual manner. And the mean whereby the Body of Christ is received and eaten in the Supper is Faith.

The Sacrament of the Lord's Supper was not by Christ's ordinance reserved, carried about, lifted up, or worshipped.

The eucharist is described here as a real but spiritual partaking of the body and blood. Transubstantiation made the partaking too literal, overthrowing its sacramental, sign-based nature. For the same reason, Catholic practices of worshipping the sacrament outside the sign-context of the liturgy are rejected.

The liturgy for holy communion expresses the same careful attention to the body and blood as a sacramental and spiritual reality, neither literal on the one hand, nor merely mental and memorial on the other, as in the prayer of humble access:

Grant us therefore, gracious Lord, so to eat the flesh of thy Son Jesus Christ, and to drink his blood, that our sinful bodies may be made clean by his body, and our souls washed through his most precious blood, and that we may evermore dwell in him, and he in us.

What looks like a literalism (based on John 6.53) is immediately followed by a metaphorical description of spiritual cleansing, and then by a description of the goal of holy communion, union with Christ, again based on John (14.20). The outward and the inner levels are neither dissociated nor confused; there is strong sense of the middle term, the sacramental reality, enabling the physical to signify and shape the spiritual.

Like many reformers, Cranmer re-emphasized the meal dimension of holy communion, which had steadily been lost since the early *agapés*. He reordered churches so that the altar became a holy table for a supper in the middle of the choir. In the eucharistic prayer the holy communion was placed, likewise, in the middle, directly after the words of institution.

Two alternative prayers now followed communion. One was the remainder of the old eucharistic prayer, a prayer of offering whose new position *after* communion made it clear that the offering was not a resacrifice of the historical Christ, but that of the whole church, having been made into the body of Christ by the act of communion. Echoing St Paul and the Fathers, this was 'a reasonable, holy and lively sacrifice' of 'praise and thanksgiving'.

The other is a prayer of thanksgiving:

> . . . that thou dost vouchsafe to feed us, who have duly received these holy mysteries, with the spiritual food of the most precious body and blood of thy Son our Saviour Jesus Christ; and dost assure us thereby . . . that we are very members incorporate in the mystical body of thy Son, which is the blessed company of all faithful people.

This makes clear Augustine's point, that our feeding on Christ assures our incorporation into his mystical body, not his incorporation into ours.

Later Anglo-Catholic theologians followed early Fathers like Justin and the theologians of Alexandria in relating the eucharist to the incarnation. As Christ was divine and human, two substances in one person, his divinity not annihilating his humanity, so, Charles Gore argued (1895, p. 283), he could be present in bread and wine without annihilating them.

Calvin: Communing with Christ in the Spirit

Like Cranmer, and Berengrar before him, Calvin believed that the ascension of Christ to the Father prevented any literal presence on earth. However, as we receive the bread and wine, the Holy Spirit fills us with grace, and as it were lifts us up to commune with Christ who is in heaven, truly to receive his body and blood spiritually there.

Zwingli: Sign and Memorial

Zwingli believed that the bread and wine were bare signs of the body and blood of Christ, and the eucharist a memorial meal in which the last supper is remembered. This meal was not grace-bearing, except in the sense that pious memories could make people more receptive to grace. The radical reformation tended to follow Zwingli, some denominations – for example the Society of Friends, or Quakers, and the Salvation Army – even dispensing with sacraments altogether, aiming for a purely spiritual worship.

Sacrifice and Presence

As well as the question of the sense in which the *body* of Christ may be said to be present in the eucharist, a related area of controversy has raged over the sense in which the *cross* of Christ is present, and whether the eucharist should be regarded as a sacrifice.

For Catholics and Orthodox, late New Testament writings such as Hebrews are taken as entitling us to see Christ's crucifixion as a sacrifice and hence importing the language of sacrifice to that event, the eucharist, where Christ is believed to be most fully present. Hence John Chrysostom readily described the eucharist in Old Testament sacrificial terms, with a hint of the heavenly slain Lamb of Revelation:

> When you see the Lord sacrificed and lying before you, and the high-priest standing over the sacrifice and praying, and all who partake being tinctured with that precious blood, can you think that you are still among men and still standing on earth? (cited in Melinsky, p. 53)

In the West, actions such as the breaking of the host were related specifically to the actions of a sacrifice; or more subtly, the presence of Christ in separated body and blood was seen as signifying the shedding of his blood from his body in his death. (The Orthodox conversely claim that in receiving the bread and wine united on a spoon, they are sharing in the risen Christ in whom body and blood are reunited.)

Here, there are two issues:

1 the presence of Christ's body and blood in the bread and wine; and
2 the presence of Christ's sacrifice on Calvary in the action of the eucharist.

There are $2 \times 2 = 4$ possibilities.

Western Catholicism regards Christ as present in both senses: the mass is a sacrifice because the bread and wine become the body and blood of Christ, in that sense being sacrificed or made holy, and the 'sacred victim' is then offered at the end of the eucharistic prayer. So the sacrifice of Calvary is re-presented and its benefits claimed and realized once more in a very real sense.

At the other extreme, for *Zwingli*, Christ would be present in neither sense, the bread and wine being bare signs, and his sacrifice being altogether complete and unrepeatable.

Luther, and some Anglicans would affirm 1 that the body and blood are there on the altar, but agree with Zwingli over the completeness of Christ's sacrifice on the cross, denying presence 2. The emphasis is on holy communion, sharing in the body and blood Christ offered once for all on Calvary.

The fourth possibility, affirming 2 and denying 1, regards the eucharist as an action in which the once for all sacrifice of Calvary is made fully present, but in the action of the eucharist as a whole, with less focus on the elements themselves. *Orthodoxy* tends in this direction, which explains how bread and wine can be adored as symbols of Christ at the Great Entrance, when Christ's heavenly sacrifice is dramatized, though this is before the consecration; while consecrated elements, though reserved for the sick, are never adored outside the drama of the liturgy. A similar view appears in Anglo-Catholic scholars like Dix, for whom the eucharist is a sacrifice because the shape of the liturgy as a whole – taking, blessing, breaking and sharing – is that of a sacrifice in which Calvary is re-presented.

Since Dix, moreover, the notion of *anamnesis* – poorly translated 'memorial' – has been viewed as implying a 'making present' of the past. It is doubtful whether the term itself necessarily implies this, but such a making present is undoubtedly implied in the Hebrew festivals that form the background of the eucharist. At the Passover every Israelite is supposed to keep the Passover as if he himself were present at the exodus from Egypt. Likewise, C. H. Dodd argued (1964, p. 234),

... at each eucharist we are *there* – we are in the night in which he was betrayed, at Golgotha, before the Empty Tomb on Easter Day, and in the upper room where he appeared; and we are at the moment of his coming, with the angels ...

This, however, suggests a spiritual reimmersion of the present in the saving past event, rather than a recalling of the past event into the present. This is a subtle distinction, but possibly vital to all who believe in Christ's complete accomplishment of salvation.

This fourth view has been for many a path of ecumenical reconciliation, such as we see in documents like ARCIC (the joint Anglican-Roman Catholic statement) and BEM (the World Council of Churches statement, referred to previously). Calvinists like Baillie have felt able to speak of the eucharist as the church's 'sacrifice of praise' in which Calvary is not repeated so much as re-presented. The late New Testament writers we have mentioned feel able to describe the church as a 'priestly people', using the term (*hiereus*) that relates to sacrifice, while never using this language of individual priests. The eucharist may then be seen as the place where the ongoing body of Christ (the church) achieves by the power of the Spirit its mystical identity with the one offering of Christ on the cross, and in that sense knows the presence of the eucharistic body of Christ acting in its midst.

Baillie therefore argues (1964, p. 121) that the mistake of medieval theology was not in its view of the mass as sacrificial, but the way the mass separated two aspects, 'first, the sacrifice of the mass, an offering by man (*sic*) to God, and then the gift of the heavenly food, Christ giving his body and blood to the communicants'. In reality, as the Dominican father Herbert McCabe writes (1964, p. 83),

... the Mass is not two things: the sacrifice of the church and the sacrifice of Christ. From one point of view it is the sacrifice of Christ because it is the sacrifice of the church – for the church's sacrificial meal, the 'breaking of bread', is the sacramental rite which shows forth and realizes the sacrifice of Christ. From another point of view it is the sacrifice of the church only because it is the sacrifice of Christ, for it is only in Christ that the church realizes herself; until the bread and wine represent Christ they do not at the deepest level represent us.

Sacrifice and Appeasement

However, controversy has arguably raged here mainly because of the kind of sacrifice that has been envisaged. Trent reaffirmed the mass as a *propitiatory* sacrifice, that is, a sacrifice that averts the wrath of God. Seeing the cross in exactly similar terms, the Protestants took their cue once again from Hebrews, and saw Christ's sacrifice as appeasing God for ever. No longer, they argued, are good works, let alone sacrifices, necessary to avert God's wrath. Catholic and Protestant alike have focused on sacrifice as a propitiation for our sins.

In this they are connecting with the lesser sacrifices that were offered for sins and impurities in the complex temple system, but above all with the scapegoat sacrifice. The last supper narratives do indeed contain a hint of such sacrifices through the mention of 'the forgiveness of sins', but against this, note that the scapegoat was sent into the desert; its blood was not shed. Those narratives relate more clearly to Passover lamb sacrifice – because of the context – and the covenant bull sacrifice. The blood of Christ is there most explicitly related to the new covenant. So surely the one sacrifice of Christ in which the church eucharistically shares should be seen not primarily as a propitiation, but rather as a Passover sacrifice leading to liberation, and a covenant sacrifice binding humanity in a new way to God.

The 'works' that bothered the reformers consisted of the plethora of rituals designed to curry favour with God. They were, of course, not against doing good works as such. If they were anxious to exclude the concept of 'offering' from the eucharist, it was because of its connection with wanting to appease God with our finery. The reformers were obviously not opposed to the natural idea of responding to God's great love with a love of our own that leads us to offer all that we are and have. Sadly in some Protestant circles these distinctions still get lost in a ritualistic obsession with eliminating any notion of offering from the eucharist; as if we could find favour with God by steadfastly refusing ever to offer him anything![2]

Modes of Presence

How can Christ be present, whether in his body or in his sacrificial act? Of course it is a mystery, but Christians need always to make sure that their mysteries are not confusions or mystifications. True mystery emerges only when we have tried our best to understand, and have come to understand that we cannot fully understand, and why. So let us see how far we can go in understanding this mystery of presence, if only to find that our wonder is increased.

We can distinguish at least four kinds of presence:

1 **Space-time or physical presence** Something is present to me if it is close to me in time and space.
2 **Sign or linguistic presence** Someone, though absent in sense 1, can be present to me in spirit or thought, through a letter, phone call or email. Conversely if someone is standing next to me facing the other way and silent, they will be present physically but absent in terms of sign.
3 **Effective or causal presence** The moon, though absent physically, is present in its effect on tides. Smoke shows the presence of fire. The departed may be present in a garden they have designed, or the books they have written, which continue to cause new feelings and thoughts.
4 **Personal presence** Someone may be present in their face or touch, in a loving rapport we share even in the absence of language.

Bodily presence seems to be a composite of 1, 2 and 3. To be bodily present, someone needs to be physically close, to be communicating with me through language or signs, and to be making things happen in the world around them which I can notice and perhaps share in. Personal presence 4 may be there too, but strangers can be bodily present without my having any sense of the person they are, like bodies on a crowded tube.

Now what about the presence of God? In Christian understanding, we note:

• The Father is present in sense 3, in that he is the fundamental cause of the universe; each thing manifests his creative power. He is present in every-thing as the ultimate reason why it is there at all. But he is not, except for a de kind of pantheist, physically present in 1 or locatable at any specific p__ce or time.

- The Son during his time on earth as Jesus Christ was present in sense 1, but this is the only time he was present in a physical way. He was also present then in sense 2, in his signs and teaching. And now? See below.
- The Holy Spirit completes 4, the presence of God to us as persons. According to the Orthodox theologian Lossky (1973, p. 167), while Christ unites his divine person to our shared human nature, the Spirit unites his divine nature to each distinctive human person. 'Christ creates the unity of His mystical body through the Holy Spirit; the Holy Spirit communicates Himself to human persons through Christ.' And the Spirit transfigures us into the restored image of God (2 Cor. 3.18), so that we begin to see God in one another's person.

So to the issue before us: In which senses could Christ be said to be present in the eucharist?

Effective sign presence

Obviously even Zwingli would accept that the eucharist is a sign which Christ has made for us, in which he can become present to our souls in sense 2.

But the creator unites to this sign presence a causal presence. As noted in Chapter 2, the Word of God is an effective, self-realizing Word. In our lives, presence is fraught with absence. When we describe something in signs we know that words are treacherous and that meanings slip, so that the real thing eludes our descriptions and we can never make sign-presence fully marry up to effective or physical presence of anything. But for Christians the flesh of Christ incarnates the Word of God. His body is the communication of the Father that cannot fail; in him effectiveness and significance coincide, the one guaranteeing the other. So the tradition that introduces the incarnation to speak of the eucharist makes a vital point; when we speak the Word of Christ, faithfully to his Word, he speaks his body, his effectiveness, in and through that Word. The eucharistic Word, being a Word of God, cannot but effect the reality it signifies. In the words of Elizabeth I, 'What God's Word doth make it, I do believe and take it.'

Here the notion of divine institution is vital, since it is the signs we have reason to believe[3] are God-given that are guaranteed to be effective in this way. Symbols of God we make on our own initiative may be helpful 'sacramentals', but they will not be sacraments because we cannot be sure they will 'do what they say'.

Bodily but not physical

This means that the eucharist is like a bodily presence, but lacking the literal physical presence we expect of bodies. This is the point that Berengrar, Cranmer and Calvin were trying to establish as against Radbert – that the literal body of Christ is in heaven. Since God is omnipresent, Christ's being with God 'in heaven' means that he is present everywhere – something none of the theologians we have considered would deny – but it also means that he is not physically in any specific place on earth, something Aquinas too was anxious to affirm when he argued that 'Christ's body is not localised in this sacrament' (1989, III.76.5, p. 579). McCabe agrees: 'Although in the sacraments Christ touches us, we do not touch him physically, because he is present only insofar as he is symbolized' (1964, p. 42).

So what of transubstantiation? Is the bread still bread, or the body of Christ? I suggest that Luther's consubstantiation makes sense, because substances can operate on different levels (see p. 72). On one level, the level on which we describe day-to-day objects, it is clearly physically bread; no scientific analysis would detect any particles of human flesh. The woman I heard of who went without holy communion because she was a vegetarian need not have worried! The eucharist does not involve cannibalism. If Radbert and strands of medieval piety suggest it does, Aquinas does not. But on a deeper level there is something else going on. By means of signs and symbols God is creating and sustaining the church through the sacrifice of Christ, enabling it to be, at the deepest level of its own reality, the body of Christ. And on this level of symbol-mediated reality, the bread and wine are the body and blood of Christ.

But again, this does not override their reality as bread and wine, but rather, perfects it. All the natural and Hebrew symbolism of bread and wine, noted previously, are taken up into this divine sacramentality. When it becomes the body of Christ, bread is the true and living Bread, broken to gather the broken world to wholeness. When it becomes the blood of Christ, wine is the true Vine, the cup of salvation, lifted up and brimming over for the life of the world.

And this implies that those who affirm a substantial change here are right – a new, substantial level emerges. So the appropriate analogies would be the way, when an artist is at work, at first there are only splashes of paint on a canvas, but in due course we can see that a painting has emerged; or at conception, when at one moment there are only wriggling sperm and egg, there then comes a point (which does not have to be precisely definable) when we have to say that a new human life is emerging; or at the transfiguration of Christ, when at one moment there is just a rabbi with strange teachings standing in prayer on a mountain, and then we can say here is the Beloved of God, shining in divine light. So it is when bread and wine come together in the eucharistic liturgy, there comes a point (not necessarily precisely definable) when we have to say, 'Here (though not physically located just here) is the body and the blood of Christ'. And though we can also say truly, 'Here are bread and wine', that is no longer an *appropriate* truth to refer to, any more than it is now anything but rude to refer to the painting as just canvas plus paint, or the embryo as just a cluster of cells. The difference, of course, is that when we do the things with bread and wine, it is God who is painting the picture of himself in us.

Personal presence

But something is still lacking. To impart a full presence, the eucharist needs to impart personal presence too. The rite itself cannot supply this. Bread and wine do not have a face or a personality we can love in a human way, even if we may adore the presence in or, better, through them.

To supply this is the work of the Spirit as described by Lossky above on p. 154. As the people receive them, the bread and wine, already effective signs bearing the sacramental presence of Christ, as just defined, release the full personal presence of Christ in his church. And it is surely in each other's face, transformed by the eucharist, that we encounter the personal presence of God. As Augustine said, what we receive is ourselves transformed in the body of Christ, such that we do not consume Christ; he subsumes us, graciously in bloodless sacrifice.

Because of this, accounts which simply regard sacraments as instruments whereby God creates 'grace' in us need to be deepened by a more personal account whereby we relate through them to the uncreated Father, through the Son in the communion of the Spirit. As McCabe writes (1964, p. 4),

> Grace does not make us a better kind of creature, it raises us beyond creaturehood, it makes us share in divinity. This share in divinity is . . . expressed by the fact that . . . we are creatures who are on speaking terms with God.

In this way the body of Christ, as it makes eucharist, becomes the full presence of Christ, in every sense but the physical. In the eucharist therefore there remains a sense in which Christ is absent – the sense in which he eluded his disciples in the bread breaking at Emmaus, and would not have Mary Magdalen hold on to his risen body (John 20.17). For total presence we must await the fullness of the kingdom when signs and sacraments shall cease.

ARCIC sums up (in 1.7 and 1.8) the many ways in which Christ is present in the whole eucharistic action, and offers himself, but it also affirms his transcendence of the sacrament.

> It is the same Lord who through the proclaimed word invites his people to his table, who through his minister presides at that table, and who gives himself sacramentally in the Body and Blood of his paschal sacrifice. It is the Lord present at the right hand of the Father, and therefore transcending the sacramental order, who thus offers to his church, in the eucharistic signs, the special gift of himself . . .
>
> When this offering is met by faith, a lifegiving encounter results. Through faith Christ's presence – which does not depend on the individual's faith in order to be the Lord's real gift of himself to his church – becomes no longer just a presence for the believer, but also a presence with him . . . We must recognize both the sacramental sign of Christ's presence

and the personal relationship between Christ and the faithful which arises from that presence.

Exercise

Reflect on these four senses of presence. In what sense do you think Christ is present:
- to everyone;
- to a Jew keeping the Passover;
- in the eucharist at the readings;
- in the eucharist after communion;
- in an act of kindness;
- in the kingdom of heaven.

Further Reading

St Augustine, 1994, *Sermons*, trans. Edmund Hill, New York: New City Press.

Gustaf Aulén, 1960, *Eucharist and Sacrifice*, Edinburgh: Oliver and Boyd.

D. M. Baillie, 1964, *The Theology of the Sacraments*, London: Faber.

Thomas Best and Dagmar Heller (eds), 2004, *Worship Today*, Geneva: WCC.

C. H. Dodd, 1964, *The Apostolic Preaching and its Developments*, London: Harper and Row.

Charles Gore, 'Transubstantiation and Nihilism', in 1895, *Dissertation on subjects connected with the Incarnation*, London: John Murray.

Charles Gore, 1907, *The Body of Christ*, London: John Murray.

David Gregg, 1976, *Anamnesis in the Eucharist*, Cambridge: Grove Books.

Franz Hildebrandt, 1967, *I Offered Christ: A Protestant study of the mass*, London: Epworth.

St Justin Martyr, 1997, *First and Second Apologies*, Mahwah and New York: Paulist Press.

Ralf Keifer, 1982, *Blessed and Broken*, Wilmington: Michael Glazier.

Vladimir Lossky, 1973, *The Mystical Theology of the Eastern Church*, Cambridge and London: James Clarke.

Herbert McCabe, 1964, *The New Creation*, London and Melbourne: Sheed and Ward.

Herbert McCabe, 1987, *God Matters*, London: Chapman.

M. A. Hugh Melinsky, 1992, *The Shape of Ministry*, Norwich: Canterbury Press.

David Power, 1987, *The Sacrifice We Offer: The Tridentine dogma and its reinterpretation*, Edinburgh: T & T Clark.

Kenneth Stevenson, 1989, *Accept this Offering: The eucharist as sacrifice today*, Collegeville, Minnesota: The Liturgical Press.

St Thomas Aquinas, 1989, *Summa Theologiae: A concise translation*, ed. Timothy McDermott, London: Eyre and Spottiswoode, and Methuen.

Max Thurian, 1983, *The Mystery of the Eucharist: An ecumenical approach*, London: Mowbray.

Rowan Williams, 1982, *Eucharistic Sacrifice: The roots of a metaphor*, Cambridge: Grove Books.

G. D. Yarnold, 1960, *The Bread which We Break*, Cambridge: Lutterworth.

Also the ecumenical books and websites listed under Chapter 5.

10

Eucharistic Theology: Space–Time, Society and Spirituality

In the previous chapter, we did some theology of the eucharist. We were, perhaps foolishly, trying to use our language and concepts drawn from our world to understand it. By the end of the chapter, however, the process had reversed; we were finding, perhaps, that thinking about the eucharist 'bent our minds', and forced us to develop our notions of presence. In other words we were beginning to move from theology of the eucharist to eucharistic theology, using the eucharist to reshape our concepts and our understanding of the world and what is possible in it.

In this chapter we will see if we can follow through that reverse movement from the eucharist back to the world. We will try accepting, or at least suspending disbelief about, the eucharist as a God-given language with which to see the world as it really is in God, in sacramental wholeness; and with which to challenge a society that falls far short of this wholeness.

This is a vast project, and we will only look here at a taster of eucharistic theology. Moving from the cosmos through the social to the personal, we begin by looking at some broad ideas amounting to a eucharistic cosmology, then move on to look at social and political challenges posed by the eucharist if we take it seriously as a model for society. Finally, we reflect on how our own piety is shaped by understandings of the eucharist implicit in our hymns.

Eucharistic Cosmology: Teilhard and Jantzen

In Chapter 5 we noted the Orthodox notion of the cosmic body of Christ, but similar ideas have been developing in the modern West. Teilhard de Chardin sought to reconcile his belief as a scientist in evolution with his theology as a Catholic priest. Unable to celebrate mass with bread and wine, he wrote 'The Mass on the World', opening with an offertory:

> Since once again, Lord – though this time not in the forests of the Aisne but in the steppes of Asia – I have neither bread, nor wine, nor altar, I will raise myself beyond these symbols, up to the pure majesty of the real itself; I, your priest, will make the whole earth my altar and on it will offer you all the labours and sufferings of the world.

Teilhard moves on through all the stages of the mass, including the words of institution:

> Do you now therefore, speaking through my lips, pronounce over this earthly travail your twofold efficacious word: the word without which all that our wisdom and our experience have built up must totter and crumble – the word through which all our most far-reaching speculations and our encounter with the universe are come together into a unity. Over every living thing which is to spring up, to grow, to flower, to ripen during this day say again the words: This is my Body. And over every death-force which waits in readiness to corrode, to wither, to cut down, speak again your commanding words which express the supreme mystery of faith: This is my Blood.

Note how the positive aspects of the world are identified with Christ's body, while the negative and painful are identified with his blood. Jesus himself spoke of the cross as the cup he had to drink (Matt. 20.22–23; Mark 10.38–39; and Matt. 26–27 – in Gethsemane), but so far as I know no tradition differentiated bread and cup in quite this way until Teilhard. The mass continues with an epiclesis of divine fire upon the earth, and proceeds to a communion with God through yet beyond all things.

Teilhard developed a perspective that saw the universe as evolving through various stages towards Christ as the omega point. However, scientists and theologians alike criticize him for using ideas that are an uneasy blend of both disciplines. In some of his other writings, perhaps, he confuses theological and biological levels, whereas in the 'Mass on the World' he uses his experience of the eucharist to unfold a deeper level of the reality that on another level is adequately described in scientific terms.

We note that the words 'This is my body' could be construed in a very literal way as a claim to divinity. Jesus could have been claiming that bread was literally part of his divine body, and that wine was blood from his divine veins. Such pantheistic notions are not quite what Teilhard intends, but are attributed to Jesus by the Gospel of Thomas:

> I am the light that is above them all. I am all things: all things came forth from me, and all things attained to me. Split a piece of wood, I am there; lift up the stone and you will find me there. (v. 77, in Morrice, 1997, p. 122)

Latterly Grace Jantzen (1984) has carefully argued from a feminist perspective that we should not regard God as a disembodied Spirit, but see the world as God's body. However, her ideas are based on a philosophical theology rather than the cosmic Christ and eucharist of Teilhard. Though mainstream theology has never seen God as essentially incarnated in a cosmic body, orthodox theology does claim that in Christ, God the Son had and continues to have a human body. By combining sacramental theology with an understanding of the incarnate Christ as the focus and goal of the cosmos (based on Paul, Irenaeus, the Orthodox Fathers and Teilhard), a sound eucharistic cosmology could emerge. So rather than assert a static pantheistic identity of the world with God's body, we could start from the eucharist and move out to a dynamic understanding of the world as *becoming* the body of Christ through the work of the Spirit in the sacramental church.

Eucharistic Subversion

But such ideas will be disembodied abstractions unless we can root them in a concrete way of transforming the actual societies we live in. So I turn to look at the ways the eucharist in itself may be said to challenge and subvert the world in the name of the kingdom. There are at least two major ways.

1 *Eucharistic koinonia* The latter word can be translated 'fellowship', 'communion' or 'sharing'. The basic notion is making things *koiné*, common to all. The earliest Christians seem to have shared more in common than the eucharistic bread and wine (Acts 2.44 and 4.32). And the whole sacrament is based on total giving of God to us and of us to God. If we resist spiritualizing this, the implication seems to be a socialism, not enforced by the state but elicited by a eucharistic church. Obviously the mainstream church has resisted this, but Anabaptists and others of the radical reformation on the one hand, and Catholic socialists and liberation theologians on the other, have supported the idea. We will explore *koinonia* a little in the next section.

2 *Eucharistic value* Imagine why someone might value an old table. One person might value it for the fine oak it is made of, with the beautiful grain, another for the wonderful craftsmanship that went into it, another for the fact that it would fetch £1,000 on the current market, another for the fact that it was inherited from his now departed father, another for its beauty, another because he has plans to use it in a new bedroom where it will fit in perfectly. Something may possess value for various reasons: for what it is made of, how it was made, what it costs, what it means personally in memories and associations, for what it can be made into, and so on. Now consider this offertory prayer, modelled on a Jewish blessing prayer and widely used across the denominations:

> Blessed are you, Lord God of all creation. Through your goodness we have this bread to offer, which earth has given and human hands have made. It will be for us the bread of life.

There is a similar prayer over the wine. The prayer moves from the raw material 'which earth has given' through the labour it represents, to what it will be made into, the bread of life. We have seen how other values accrue to the bread and wine, including the memory of the past, but conspicuously missing is market value. It makes no difference to the eucharist whether we use cheap homemade wine or a costly vintage port.

Could the eucharist itself represent a challenge to a culture that seems to value only what it can measure and market? What would our world be like, if it celebrated value eucharistically, counting market value no value at all? And if in our buying we paid more attention to whether the earth is being cared for, labour properly remunerated, and the values of God respected?

Discussion

Discuss these questions.

We will turn to the eucharist as a way of combating prevailing ideology on p. 167.

Eucharist, Koinonia and Kingdom: Zizioulas

The rediscovery of eschatology – the last things and the kingdom of God – is perhaps the most significant twentieth-century contribution to eucharistic theology. Teilhard with his stress on Christ as omega point was of course eschatological in his own way, while Geoffrey Wainwright (1979) has made major contributions, but I turn to Greek Orthodox theologian John Zizioulas, and his understanding of the kingdom as creating the church through the eucharist.

Taking his cue from the Trinity, Zizioulas sees people as being created by their relationships, before they create them themselves. In the same way, he argues, the church is created by, rather than creating, the eucharistic communion (*koinonia*):

We [must] give up envisaging the eucharist as . . . a 'means of grace' 'used' or 'administered' by the church. The ancient understanding of the eucharist – common in its general lines until about the twelfth century to both East and West – was very different . . . It was in the eucharist that the church would contemplate her eschatological nature, would taste the very life of the Holy Trinity; in other words she would realize man's true being as image of God's own being . . . Thus the eucharist was not the act of a pre-existing church; it was an event *constitutive* of the being of the church. (1993, pp. 20–1)

For Zizioulas, the Holy Spirit creates the church through the eucharist, which is the feast of the end time. Zizioulas describes the church, paradoxically, as a tree growing from the end of time, and as 'the memory of the future' (p. 180).

This perspective is different equally from the Zwinglian emphasis on memory of the past, and from theologies that see the church as a continuation of the incarnation or an apostolic past. For Zizioulas, the eucharist 'confronts history with a presence from beyond history . . . the presence of the Kingdom here and now' (p. 174). So in the eucharist a new society is created over against the world. At the Orthodox liturgy there is often a palpable sense of this interruption of historical time by the end time, dramatized in the 'entrances' sweeping from the hidden sanctuary beyond into the midst of the people, and in the candle-lit cloud of saints, our contemporaries in the kingdom, watching from the icons.

Sacraments and the Making of the Church

It may be worth pausing to suggest that it is not only the eucharist but the sacraments as a whole that create the church, and to test out how the church might be said to derive its essential qualities from Christ through them. A useful characterization of the church lies in the four 'marks' listed in the article of the Nicene Creed: 'I believe in *one, holy, catholic and apostolic* Church.' Let us consider these in turn.

- *Oneness or unity* Christ prayed to the Father that his followers 'may be one, even as we are one' (John 17.11). So unity is a peace the church brings to the world through unity with the one God. It is not a uniformity that comes from conformity to an institution, but the gift of God, not least in the holy communion that unites many in one body of Christ. But when human sin destroys unity and divides us, the sacrament of reconciliation is there to reunite us. Unity is also expressed in a special way in the *koinonia* of marriage, where two different people share one 'flesh', one life together, like a little church.

- *Holiness* The church as an institution or congregation is certainly sinful, but is given a holiness by being united to the only Holy One, Christ, in holy communion. The less concerned it is with its own institutional power or moral purity, the more this holiness will shine through. Again, the church has a way of restoring holiness when threatened or broken by disease or psychic disorder, through the sacrament of healing. Indeed the words 'holy', 'whole' and 'heal' come from the same ancient Germanic root *hael*.

- The *catholicity* of the church means its 'universal' embracing of humanity. It is given in baptism, the sacrament of our participation in humanity redeemed by the dying and rising of Christ. This is the one sacrament Christians universally acknowledge as valid across the denominations; though sadly, some still draw the boundaries of the 'universal' church more narrowly than this common baptism.

- The *apostolicity* of the church means its faithfulness to the teaching of the apostles and its being 'sent' into the world with the message of Christ as the apostles were. Some traditions add to this the 'apostolic succession' of bishops that is traced back to the apostles (see Chapter 12). All would see apostolicity as maintained, nurtured and guided by the ordination of ministers responsible for the deliverance of Word and Sacrament. And we have seen that confirmation or chrismation can be viewed as handing on to each Christian a share in the apostolic teaching and mission, symbolized in episcopal churches by the role of the bishop as joining the confirmed to the lineage of the apostles, as he lays on their heads his apostolic hands.

Discussion

Discuss the above suggestions, and possible criticisms, for example by those who would regard apostolicity as given in baptism, and those who would only see two sacraments as essential to the church.

Eucharist Against Ideology

Now let us look more closely at the way the eucharist challenges worldly values and ideologies.

Herbert McCabe describes the eucharist as the language of the kingdom (cf. 'Sacramental Language' in his 1987). In the fallen world, he argues, words never effect what they signify. At best they can effect an intention to mean something which we hope someone will recognize. Language is full of deception and misconception, and fraught with the absence of the thing from the word. Our words of love can never really express the fullness of our being to another. But in the eucharist, Christ does precisely that, speaking words that effect the very love and communion they signify, as it were speaking his very being into ours.

We may enlarge on this. Normal language is full of ideology, words that say one thing and effect another. The primary Marxist example is the way an exchange of work for a wage 'says' that the two people are freely agreeing to a contract as equals. What the exchange effects may be a situation of dire exploitation by the employer of the worker, who may be compelled by poverty to accept the meagre wage she apparently freely contracts into, which is always less than the value, in other senses, of what she makes or does.

Not only that, but the misrepresentation of the effect by the sign actually helps effect and perpetuate the inequality, because if people saw the inequality for what it was, they would condemn it. (Here, I am using 'sign' in the broad sense of any meaning-bearing human act, be it an action, a word, or a visual symbol.) So we can define an ideology as a sign or set of *signs that effect the evil they falsely signify*, and moreover, effect or perpetuate the evil *by means of the false signification*.

Note that ideology is neither a simple lie nor a straightforward delusion. In a lie there is an intended mismatch between a *sign* and *reality*, and in delusion there is an unnoticed mismatch between *belief* and *reality*, whereas in ideology the mismatch is between *sign* and the *effect* of making or saying it. Ideology can be true. For instance I may say 'The sufferings of the poor detach them from worldly greed, ennoble their spirit, and make them more likely to enter heaven than us rich.' And this may be neither a deliberate lie nor a self-delusion (though, of course, it could be both!). But saying it might misrepresent the evils of oppression as being good for the poor, and by that means encourage people to perpetuate the oppression.

But now recall the definition of a sacrament as a sign that effects the sacred reality it signifies. The truth and lucidity of a sacrament are themselves part of the means by which it is so effective, so usable by God. Aquinas defines sacraments as *signs that effect the sacred reality they signify*, and moreover, that the way the sacred reality is effected is *by means of its signification* in the sacrament.

If this is true, a sacrament is the opposite of ideology, and potentially its undoing. The eucharist starts to build a new community based not only on truth, but on the entire absence of ideology: a society that is entirely lucid as to reality. In it, good appears simply as good, the free gift of God through the Son. At the same time evil appears for what it is, in bread broken and wine poured out, as the crucifying of this gift. And yet evil and death become precisely that through which God's goodness and life is given. The dark forms of torture and death are overcome in the transparent and bloodless sharing of God's being with our own. Or so William Cavanaugh argues (1998), seeing the eucharist as a bloodless parody of victimization and sacrifice. The body is broken in bread and the blood poured out in wine without any killing, challenging our need to torture, subdue and crucify the bodies of others.

Finally, sacraments are not just pious statements of belief and hope. If they functioned just as pious ideas, they could not overcome ideology and help us live together in justice and truth. But sacraments are rites. We have seen that rites are repeated transactions that join the ordinary to the holy, root us in the past and give us a future, and unite individuals into a society. They do so powerfully. Rites that anchor us in delusory pasts and hopes, or name the wrong things as holy, can create powerfully oppressive societies. But if there is such a thing as a eucharistic rite, as here described, it will be a uniquely powerful force for creating a good, honest and just society.

Discussion

Discuss whether you think the eucharist can be liberating in this way. Do you think the context in which, or the way in which, it is celebrated, makes a difference to the liberating power? If so, how?

Eucharistic Theology in Worship

Sacraments like the eucharist form us and our communities for good, and sign our path in life in ways that bring understanding. But perhaps they can do the opposite too. By examining the eucharistic theologies implicit in the following verses, readers are invited to become aware of how they may have been eucharistically shaped, and so begin to define their own spirituality in relation to the eucharist.

Exercise

Consider the following hymns and poems.
Which of these eucharistic theologies do they presuppose:
- memorial of supper
- presence of Christ
- union with Christ
- communion with others
- sacrifice
- transubstantiation
- the cosmic Christ
- challenges to society
- the hope of the kingdom?

And which best expresses what you would want to say?

---

1 It semes white and is red;
　It is quike and semes dede;
　It is fleshe and semes bred;
　It is on and semes too;
　It is God body and no mo.[1]

2 Love bade me welcome: yet my soul drew back,
　　Guiltie of dust and sinne.
　But quick-eyed love, observing me grow slack
　　From my first entrance in,
　Drew nearer to me, sweetly questioning,
　　If I lack'd any thing.

A guest, I answer'd, worthy to be here:
    Love said, You shall be he.
I the unkinde, ungratefull? Ah my deare,
    I cannot look on thee.
Love took my hand, and smiling did reply,
    Who made the eyes, but I?

Truth, Lord, but I have marr'd them: let my shame
    Go where it doth deserve.
And know you not, sayes Love, who bore the blame?
    My deare, then I will serve.
You must sit downe, sayes Love, and taste my meat:
    So I did sit and eat.[2]

3 Thee we adore, O hidden Saviour, thee,
who in thy sacrament dost deign to be;
both flesh and spirit at thy presence fail,
yet here thy presence we devoutly hail.

O blest memorial of our dying Lord,
who living bread to men doth here afford!
O may our souls for ever feed on thee,
and thou, O Christ, for ever precious be.

Fountain of goodness, Jesu, Lord and God,
cleanse us, unclean, with thy most cleansing blood;
increase our faith and love, that we may know
the hope and peace which from thy presence flow.

O Christ, whom now beneath a veil we see,
may what we thirst for soon our portion be:
to gaze on thee unveiled, and see thy face,
the vision of thy glory and thy grace.[3]

4 Victim Divine, thy grace we claim
While thus thy precious death we show;

Once offered up, a spotless Lamb,
In thy great temple here below,
Thou didst for all mankind atone,
And standest now before the throne.

Thou standest in the holiest place,
As now for guilty sinners slain;
Thy blood of sprinkling speaks and prays
All-prevalent for helpless man;
Thy blood is still our ransom found,
And spreads salvation all around.

We need not now go up to heaven
To bring the long-sought Saviour down;
Thou art to all already given,
Thou dost e'en now thy banquet crown:
To every faithful soul appear,
And show thy real presence here.[4]

5 In bread we bring you, Lord, our bodies' labour.
In wine we offer you our spirits' grief.
We do not ask you, Lord, who is my neighbour?
But stand united now, one in belief.
Oh, we have gladly heard your Word, your holy Word,
and now in answer, Lord, our gifts we bring.
Our selfish hearts make true, our failing faith renew,
our lives belong to you, our Lord and King.

The bread we offer you is blessed and broken,
and it becomes for us our spirits' food.
Over the cup we bring your Word is spoken;
make it your gift to us your healing blood.
Take all that daily toil plants in our heart's poor soil
take all we start and spoil, each hopeful dream,
the chances we have missed, the graces we resist,
Lord, in thy Eucharist, take and redeem.[5]

6 An upper room did our Lord prepare
  for those he loved until the end;
  and his disciples still gather there
  to celebrate their risen friend.

  A lasting gift Jesus gave his own:
  to share his bread, his loving cup.
  Whatever burdens may bow us down
  he by his cross shall lift us up.

  And after supper he washed their feet,
  for service too is sacrament.
  In him our joy shall be made complete –
  sent out to serve, as he was sent.

  No end there is! We depart in peace.
  He loves beyond our uttermost:
  in every room in our Father's house
  he will be there, as Lord and host.[6]

7 The time was early evening,
  the place a room upstairs;
  the guests were the disciples
  together saying prayers.

  O, the food comes from the baker,
  the drink comes from the vine,
  the words come from the Savour:
  I will meet you in bread and wine.

  The company of Jesus
  had met to share a meal,
  but he who made them welcome
  had much more to reveal.

The bread and body broken,
the wine and blood outpoured,
the cross and kitchen table
are one by my sign and word.

On both sides of the table,
on both sides of the grave,
the Lord joins those who love him
to serve them and to save.

Lord Jesus, now among us,
Confirm our faith's intent,
As, with your words and actions,
We unite in this sacrament.[7]

10 Ah you whose body bread is, and blood
is Life itself, you offer us your broken
being in the world, your cup
of love, and pact.

　　　But can we honour
the celebration as the last
　　　night falls, and reaches out
the taking hand and kiss, to break
the indecipherable beauty of your most whole
and blessed face?

Soon you will be
nestling in crucifying hands:
bird of a new time, flying – had we but hearts
to hold you – to us in blood and body.[8]

> ## Exercise
>
> Discuss which are the most important aspects of the eucharist for you personally. Then in groups or individually, make something that expresses these aspects. It can be a hymn, a poem, a picture or a statement of faith. It does not have to be a masterpiece – a pastiche of the hymns you like is quite all right – so long as it gets across your thoughts and feelings about the eucharist.

Dimensions of the Eucharist

Figure 7 sums up what we have learnt about the eucharist. The sacrament is rooted in our organic need to eat, so that other beings have to be sacrificed in order that we may live. So humble is our God that in Christ he meets us at this level of need; the sacrifice of the cross bears fruit as we feed on Christ in bread and wine. So he establishes the church as a holy communion, united and rendered holy while yet sinful, just as were those sinners who shared his open table fellowship. He fulfils their deepest longings and ours for the friendship of God. The sacrament takes up the liberating themes of Passover sacrifice, pointing the way to society's liberation in the *agapé* or love-feast of the kingdom; it bears away the sinful barriers we build against God, and establishes the new and bloodless covenant, in which we dwell in Christ, and he in us.

Figure 7. Dimensions of the Eucharist.

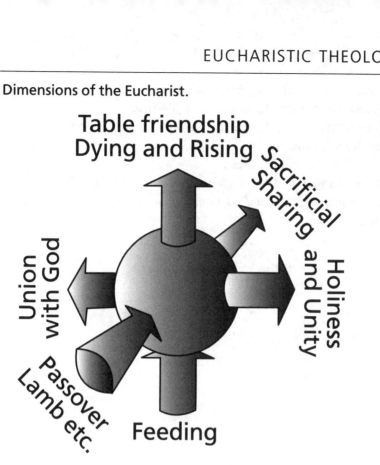

Table friendship
Dying and Rising
Sacrificial
Sharing
Union
with God
Holiness
and Unity
Passover
Lamb etc.
Feeding

Further Reading

Tissa Balasuriya, 1977, *The Eucharist and Human Liberation*, London: SCM Press.

William T. Cavanaugh, 1998, *Torture and Eucharist*, Oxford: Blackwell.

Pierre Teilhard de Chardin, 1961, *Hymn of the Universe*, New York: Harper and Row.

Kenith A. David, 1994, *Sacrament and Struggle: Signs and instruments of grace from the downtrodden*, Geneva: World Council of Churches.

Richard Giles, 1999, *Re-Pitching the Tent*, Norwich: Canterbury Press.

Richard Giles, 2004, *Creating Uncommon Worship*, Norwich: Canterbury Press.

Donald Gray, 1986, *Earth and Altar: The evolution of the parish communion in the Church of England to 1945*, Norwich: Canterbury Press.

A. G. Herbert, 1961, *Liturgy and Society*, London: Faber.

Grace Jantzen, 1984, *God's World, God's Body*, London: Darton, Longman and Todd.

G. Martelet, 1976, *The Risen Christ and the Eucharistic World*, London: Collins.

Herbert McCabe, 1987, *God Matters*, London: Chapman.

Paul McPartlan, 1993, *The Eucharist Makes the Church: Henri de Lubac and John Zizioulas in dialogue*, Edinburgh: T & T Clark.

William Morrice, 1997, *The Hidden Sayings of Jesus*, London: SPCK.

Alexander Schmemann, 1987, *The Eucharist: Sacrament of the kingdom*, New York: St Vladimir's Seminary Press.

Geoffrey Wainwright, 1979, *Eucharist and Eschatology*, London: Epworth.

John Zizioulas, 1993, *Being as Communion*, New York: St Vladimir's Seminary Press.

Part 5

Making and Remaking Church: Other Sacraments and Symbols

11

Symbols of Restoration: Reconciliation, Healing and Deliverance

Having explored the two dominical sacraments in depth, we explore briefly the others, which are recognized as sacraments by the Orthodox and Catholic but not the Protestant churches. The remaining five rites are all carried out by the mainstream Protestant churches (except that many have abandoned reconciliation), but they are regarded as pastoral offices rather than sacraments.

Two, Seven or How Many?

We have already noted reasons for not regarding them as sacraments. In the words of the Book of Common Prayer, Article 25, 'they have *not any visible sign or ceremony ordained of God*'. Either there is no obvious visible sign at all, or there is a sign that Christ is not recorded as instituting.

However, these signs clearly express the overall will of Christ in the life of the church. He inspired people, commissioned apostles, loved people, healed and forgave, and clearly wanted this work to go on in some form. In addition, they have long been part of the tradition of the church, mostly since apostolic times. For these reasons Catholics and Orthodox regard them as instituted by Christ as Lord of the church, even if there is no evidence of him having verbally instituted them in his earthly life.

Even by Catholics and Orthodox Christians, baptism and the eucharist are singled out as the great, 'dominical sacraments'. Baptism is the first, initiating sacrament, and the eucharist is the ultimate sacrament to which all the others move. So the others are either once for all extensions of baptismal vocation, or repeatable sacraments enabling or deepening full participation in the eucharist. I will call the former the sacraments or signs of vocation, which I will deal with in the next chapter, and the latter the sacraments or signs of restoration, which I deal with in this.

Confirmation extends the dimension of commitment and the gift of the Spirit which are parts of baptism, while ordination focuses in a particular, ministerial vocation the royal priesthood imparted in baptism. Reconciliation is both a renewal of the repentance of baptism, and an intensification of the penitential rite that in the West introduces the eucharist. Healing and marriage in different ways focus the holiness of life and unity with Christ which are the goal of the eucharist. If this is remembered, then we can avoid saying that those churches that acknowledge only the two sacraments are in any way lacking the fullness of life in response to the fullness of Christ, which we shall be exploring in terms of the seven.

Sacraments have traditionally been ranked either in a linear time sequence, beginning with baptism; or in a circle, centring on the eucharist. The scheme I prefer combines both into a chalice shape (Figure 8). Here baptism and eucharist have pride of place, the one as the foot on which all the others stand, the other as the chalice bowl itself which all serve to hold. On the stem is confirmation, which with baptism below and eucharist above, belongs to the process of initiation. On the left are the sacraments of restoration which can be seen as a handle supporting and leading back into the chalice, while on the right, where one might imagine the chalice spilling over into the whole of life, are the sacraments of vocation.

Here and throughout these last two chapters, wherever the word 'sacrament' appears in reference to the 'other five', Protestants are invited to read 'symbol', 'rite' or 'pastoral office'. Significantly, this will not result in any serious loss of meaning in the discussion.

Figure 8. Ordering of the Sacraments: Chalice Shape.

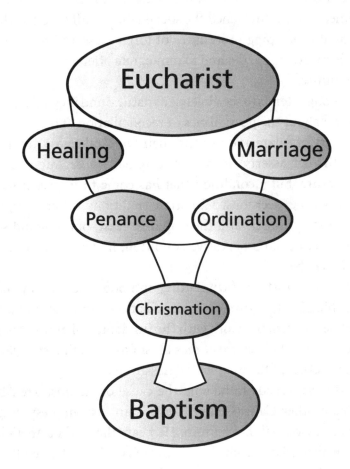

Sin and Forgiveness in the Hebrew Bible

Whether one ascribes sin to a 'fall' from an initially peaceable state, or to an aggressive and assertive nature deriving from a 'selfishness' in our genes that has assured their survival, any human society has to manage large degrees of violence and strife if it is to survive as a coherent society. So all societies have developed systems of law, which define and punish behaviour that threatens to disrupt it. Initially there was not much distinction between ritual impurity and crime, as both threatened the social fabric. Sadly societies have been less efficient at developing procedures of forgiveness and reconciliation to bring together warring parties and to reintegrate offenders and the 'unclean' into communities.

Modern thought tends to see violence as natural and inevitable,[1] and hence to be sceptical about the possibilities of reconciliation and peace. However, even if the story of Adam and Eve and their fall is taken as a myth, it seems to be a myth that asserts sin as not 'original' (*pace* Augustine) to our God-given nature, but a condition that has come to imprison us through catastrophic wrong decisions. Christian traditions differ here, with the Orthodox most optimistic and the Calvinist least, but it would seem that while sin is a serious and pervasive condition, it can never be regarded as natural or inevitable.

Sin is always against our own nature, and hope must always be pinned on the possibilities of forgiveness, reconciliation and restoration, as things that cannot be coerced, but work with the fundamental grain of our created nature. Hence the Old Testament sees all sin as involving sin against God, since it is a rejection of the nature God has given us.

So God is always ready to take up the cause of victims, like Abel, murdered by his brother Cain (Gen. 4.2–16). Cain disowns responsibility for his brother, but God will not let him. He hears the 'cry' of Abel's blood for vengeance, which arises 'from the ground'. Cain has offended the ground, the earth God has created. However, God does not avenge the crime with an equivalent punishment. Though he must suffer, Cain is allowed to live, and is even protected by God from those who would seek vengeance. This balance of justice and mercy is typical of God's dealings with humans in the Old Testament, and is what we find emerging in the sacrament of reconciliation at its best.

Because all sin involves God in this way, forgiveness of sin is ascribed in the Old Testament to God alone, though it also involves restitution to those harmed. Hebrew law contained many rites to atone for individual sin and impurity, generally involving sacrifice. It also provided, for the sins of the whole community, the one great ceremony of the Day of Atonement, a rite which as noted in Chapter 2 reflects the way societies so often deal with sin and reconcile divisions through a 'scapegoat' everyone can agree to punish.

Jesus and Forgiveness

In this perspective Jesus, by his wounds, is the ultimate healer, and by his death the ultimate bringer of reconciliation and peace. But his life was no less dedicated to healing and forgiveness. He scandalized the authorities by pronouncing the forgiveness of sins that only God can give. His table fellowship with sinners, and the woman's washing of Jesus' feet with her tears (Luke 7.36–50), were in a sense early sacraments of reconciliation. His actions and parables tell of an urgent ingathering to the kingdom that left no time for ritual propriety. With Zacchaeus (Luke 19.1–10) and others, forgiveness – as manifested in Jesus' desire for table fellowship – comes first, and elicits repentance, reversing the conventional order.

Early in the church, disciplines of punishment and forgiveness were felt to be necessary, and Paul (1 Cor. 5.1–13) writes of a church discipline of penalty and reconciliation. A similar discipline is found at Matthew 18.15–18, which reads like good modern disciplinary procedure, requiring that parties try to sort out issues with each other. Excommunication is the last resort, and in this context we hear: 'whatever you bind on earth will be bound in heaven, and whatever you loose on earth will be loosed in heaven' (v. 18). The saying about binding and loosing has been understood as implying that Jesus passed on to the church his divine authority to loose or absolve, and to bind or excommunicate (or perhaps to 'bind' the demons that possess the sinner). The same authority is passed on along with the 'keys of the kingdom of heaven' to Peter specifically in Matthew 16.19, and to the twelve disciples, along with the gift of the Holy Spirit, in John 20.21–23. Such passages are key to the justification of the later sacrament of penance or reconciliation, but they all reflect an institutional church that has already been established, rather than, probably, the original words of Jesus.

The above passage (Matthew 18) is almost immediately followed in verses 21–22 with Jesus saying to Peter that he must forgive 'seventy times seven'. This is then clarified (vv. 23–35) by the frightening parable of the unforgiving servant, which relates God's forgiveness of us to our forgiveness of others. Jesus was very harsh on those who fail to forgive others, but he is never recorded as having withheld forgiveness when asked. Jesus is not inviting his followers to count up wrongs until, on the 491st offence, they are entitled to vengeance! Rather, they are to use his authority to forgive, not to condemn.

Development of Penitential Discipline

By the patristic period church discipline provided a solemn, public act of confession and reconciliation for those who had committed 'capital' or 'mortal' sins. These were sins against the ten commandments, and in particular, idolatry or apostasy, adultery, or murder. After confession a period of penance – sometimes lifelong – would be imposed, a punishment for sin, which was often extremely severe.

> The lot of the penitents was not a happy one, nor was it meant to be. Not only were they expected to demonstrate their remorse 'with downcast eyes and mournful faces,' but they were also marked out as sinners by what they sometimes had to wear: sackcloth made of goat hair, to symbolize their separation from the sheep of Christ's flock; chains, to signify their bondage to sin; tags, to dramatize their poverty of virtue. Some had to cut their hair short like slaves, to show that they were slaves to Satan; others had to sprinkle themselves with ashes, to show they were spiritually dead like Adam, and cast out from the paradise of the church. Of course as public sinners they were not allowed to share in the 'communion of saints', that is, the eucharist. (Martos, 2001, p. 288)

At the end of this ordeal, according to Cyprian, the bishop would lay hands on the penitent as a sign of reconciliation achieved. Later, Athanasius describes the laying on of hands in more instrumental terms, as the actual accomplishment of reconciliation. There was no second chance, if the sinner returned to his or her evil ways; the penance was understood as a 'second plank' thrown to sinners who had lost their grip on the 'first plank' of baptism and were drowning in the sea of sin. There was no third plank.

Towards Personal Confession

These practices died out, however. Their extreme rigour, the obvious stigma, and the lack of a third chance meant that people deferred resorting to them. And when the empire became Christian, secular forces were trusted with matters of justice and penalty. The church's own discipline accordingly relaxed. More than one penance was allowed (from 584 in the West) while the East permitted confession to a spiritual guide, who could be a monk rather than a priest.

Penance was moving from the domain of law to that of spiritual nurture. Starting from the fifth century, beginning in the context of Irish monasticism, which was steeped in the desert tradition of spiritual direction, a more pastoral discipline spread, involving regular confession. The congregational prayers for the sinner dropped out, and steadily the sacrament became a private, regular discipline. In 1215 in the West this was made a prerequisite for adults at least once a year, before receiving holy communion. A priest would hear confession from a kneeling penitent, impose a penance, then pronounce absolution.

This is a sacrament where the sign and sacramental reality have never been clear. Sometimes the penance imposed was seen as penalty or punishment, but absolution preceded it, and it tended to become rather a token of true repentance. Aquinas saw it as a way of dealing with the remnants of sin repented of, including bad habits and what we would today term complexes, not a way of earning grace but a way of burning away the dark impurity that sin leaves in the soul. He believed (as did Cranmer later) that perfect repentance (truly being sorry) was essential for the sacrament to be effective. Confessing a sin one was intending to commit again would not therefore lead to forgiveness, let alone confessing a sin and being absolved in advance, for example on the way to a brothel (a medieval practice the church was quick to condemn!).

However others, such as Duns Scotus, regarded the words of absolution as effective *ex opere operato*, irrespective of subjective intention; they alone 'caused' forgiveness, and an imperfect repentance for bad reasons (for example, so as to be able to go on sinning without fear of consequence) did not prevent their being effective. This detachment of absolution from penitence opened the way for much that the Reformation would regard as abuses. For example, the church could now remit, with 'indulgences', the punishments due in purgatory.

In the East, meanwhile, confession has remained to this day more pastoral than juridical in intent. The sinner stands with the priest facing a cross and an icon of Christ. The liturgy avoids the 'I absolve you' form, and expresses Christ's forgiveness, rather than the priest's absolution on the authority given by Christ. The sins of the penitent are sacramentally 'covered' or 'hidden' by the priest's stole. However, the Roman practice of requiring confession before communion has become widespread, even as the Roman Catholic Church has relaxed this requirement.

The reformers rejected the Roman practice, for three reasons. It gave the priesthood a mediating power between humanity and God, where Christ alone should be sufficient. The imposed penance looked suspiciously like a work where the penitent strove to achieve forgiveness, rather than putting her faith in Christ. And of course the abuses connected with the sale of indulgences regarding purgatory were key triggers of the Reformation. Nevertheless, confession remained an optional part of Lutheran and Calvinist tradition, understood as effective by virtue of the saving power of the cross received in faith by the penitent. The priest was not indispensable, and honest confession to a layperson was regarded as equally valuable.

Meanwhile, in Anglican discipline, private confession and absolution formed part of the visitation of the sick, where the western Roman 'I absolve thee' form is retained. In all the Protestant churches, however, the practice of private confession gradually fell into disuse, tending to be replaced by a strong emphasis on penitence in the corporate liturgies, and self-examination in preparation for the (often quarterly) services of holy communion. In the Church of England, private confession finally lapsed only during the eighteenth century, and in the following century the Anglo-Catholic movement revived the practice.

Confession and Therapy

In the nineteenth and twentieth centuries secular developments of confession – psychotherapy and counselling – began to establish themselves. The therapeutic power of naming unconscious forces replaced confession of sin; the 'unconditional positive regard' of the counsellor replaced absolution; and the suggestion of ways of living so as to contradict complexes replaced 'penance'. The church has in turn learned from these practices, of which it was arguably a major root.

So Vatican II relaxed the requirement of confession before holy communion, and confession often became less formal, with greater emphasis on discernment and counsel. The understanding of sin itself has moved towards greater attention to the complexes and compulsions that limit freewill, and greater understanding of structural and corporate, rather than purely individual, dimensions of sin, introducing considerations of healing and deliverance (see below). Theologically, for Vatican II the penitent's contrition, confession and penance, as with Aquinas, are now viewed as the outward sign, but reconciliation with the church – the corporate dimension – is seen as the 'sacramental reality', while reconciliation with God is the ultimate reality of the sacrament. Corporate services of reconciliation have therefore been introduced, in which people confess privately in the context of a corporate act of penitential worship.

The recent Church of England *Common Worship* contains rich resources for corporate penitence and absolution but none specifically for reconciliation of a penitent. Other churches in the Anglican Communion provide beautiful examples. Thus the *American Book of Common Prayer* (1997, p. 451) contains resonances of baptism and the parable of the prodigal son, in the confession:

> Holy God, heavenly Father, you formed me from the dust in your image and likeness, and redeemed me from sin and death by the cross of your Son Jesus Christ. Through the water of baptism you clothed me with the shining garment of his righteousness, and established me among your children in your kingdom. But I have squandered the inheritance of your saints, and have wandered far in a land that is waste . . .

The dismissal echoes the prodigal's father (Luke 15.24):

> Now there is rejoicing in heaven; for you were lost, and are found; you were dead, and are now alive in Christ Jesus our Lord. Go in peace. The Lord has put away all your sins.

Here we witness a note that this sacrament has often lost, which Dietrich Bonhoeffer (1954, p. 90) described as 'the renewal of the joy of baptism'. One wonders whether if a shared and fundamentally joyful rite of reconciliation were available in the English churches, there would be the demand for 're-baptism' that there seems to be.

> ## Discussion
>
> Discuss in groups together: Is there a place for penance in the church, and if so which practice do you prefer:
> - public reconciliation for serious offences as in the patristic period;
> - regular private confession to a priest, as in the Roman Catholic tradition;
> - optional confession to the priest, as in Orthodoxy, Anglicanism and contemporary Catholicism;
> - confession to a spiritual guide who may not be ordained, as in the reformers;
> - confession and absolution by the priest at every service.

Criminal Justice and Reconciliation

Most of this history shows a steady move from the corporate to the personal in the use of this sacrament. However, our criminal justice system seems increasingly to focus on punishment rather than reconciliation and restoration, while society as a whole increasingly resorts to the scapegoat mechanism, finding people to blame for every misfortune, and tending more and more to draw lines around itself that perpetually exclude the stranger as well as the offender.[2] One wonders whether the church has something profound to offer in its old disciplines of repentance. Was the church too quick to surrender such disciplines to the state, and could they now offer a controlled way whereby the shame in crime could be both acknowledged and laid aside in a process of reconciliation with victims and restoration to society as a whole? Or has society in practice moved too far into a post-Christian order where examination of one's own conscience is abnormal, there is no sense of the universality of sin, and sin is always the other person's problem, to be punished but not redeemed?

Discussion

Discuss these issues.

Dimensions of Reconciliation

See Figure 9. The struggle for life often creates conflicts that society needs to resolve; this sacrament does so by reconciling us to Christ who befriended sinners, and took our violence into himself to bring us to peace. Spiritually, penance relates to the active renunciation of the addictions and clutter that can be a barrier against God; it restores unity to church and community. It

Figure 9. Dimensions of Reconciliation.

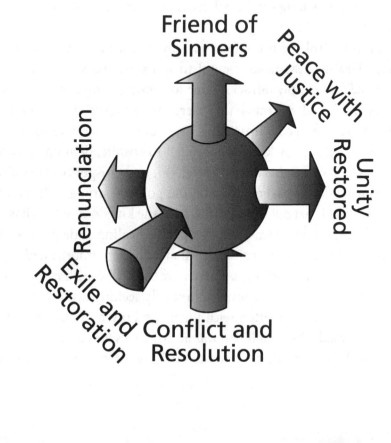

recalls the exile, in which the people of God, having lost their homeland, relived their honeymoon with God in the wilderness; so the tears of penance renew the innocent joy of baptism, and bring us home to the Father as they create justice and peace.

We now turn to the closely related sacrament of anointing for healing.

Healing and Cosmic Conflict

The olive is, along with the grape, a characteristic fruit of the Mediterranean area, but while the grape is sweet and intoxicating, the olive is sober and bitter and practical, its oil useful for lamps, for cooking, and as an ointment. If the grape connotes passion, festivity and ecstasy, the olive connotes sobriety, work and wisdom.

Olive oil has a natural healing role; before the advent of plasters and antiseptics, it was the best way to protect a wound from the air and infection. So the disciples were not innovators when they anointed and healed the sick (Mark 6.13), nor was James in his advice to pray and anoint for healing and forgiveness (James 5.14–16).

Note the close link with confession, however, which brings in a wider dimension. Healing was fundamental to Jesus' ministry, but his healing works were neither simply miracles done to impress people, nor only works of compassion, though of course they were that. In Jesus' time sickness was experienced as evil and contaminating. The sick were therefore socially outcast and marginalized. Sickness was related to cosmic, demonic powers in the same way that we might sometimes relate it to socio-political malaise. So Jesus' healing work was part of a cosmic and political struggle: 'If it is by the finger of God that I cast out the demons, then the kingdom of God has come to you' (Luke 11.20). Jesus was bringing people healing as deliverance from the powers – whether cosmic or social – that held them imprisoned.

He worked in two distinct ways. There were those whose illness was viewed as punishment. They came to Jesus voluntarily seeking healing, and he responded with forgiveness, often with touch, and often declaring that their own faith had made them well. He was acting in a sense as a sacrament for their own healing. Then there were those whose (often mental) illness was attributed to evil powers that had actually seized control. Here, typically, the person resists healing and struggles with Jesus, until he casts the demons out.

By the time of the Gospel of John, this sense of struggle had become internalized as a total warfare between the children of light and those of darkness. The healings have become signs (see Chapter 3). So Jesus' healing of the blind man is sacramental of his power to dispel spiritual blindness, which the children of darkness resist.

Finally, note that 'salvation' comes from a Latin root meaning 'healing', while the original Greek *sozo* denotes rescue and saving from death in both physical and spiritual senses. Christ's 'saving' work on the cross can be seen as the final overcoming of the powers of darkness, and the ultimate healing. He is broken and wounded that we may be whole and well. Those engaged in deep prayer and the ministry of healing speak in similar terms of taking into themselves the hurt of others, carrying forward this saving work of the crucified.

The Fall and Rise of Sacramental Healing

As in early Christianity the kingdom hope receded, so did the ministry of healing, perhaps because of its association with the conflicts of the end time. Hippolytus supplied a prayer for blessing of oil, to be used by lay folk in healing, but by and large there was little attention to such anointing by the Fathers until the fifth century, when there was some growth in what remained, as in James, a lay-administered process. There was then a distinct deathbed *viaticum* rite consisting of sacramental confession, anointing for deliverance from sin, and holy communion, administered by priests. In the Dark Ages this fused with the healing rite, and in twelfth-century simplifications in the West the prayers for healing were removed, leaving a priest-administered rite of extreme unction, to prepare the dying for death. It was this sacrament that Albertus Magnus and Thomas Aquinas described as having the grace of eliminating the vestiges of sin after confession, and preparing for entry into heaven.

The Reformers tended to regard anointing for healing as a ministry that died after the apostolic age. Calvin rejected the sacrament, and it was omitted from the Anglican Visitation of the Sick. The Council of Trent reaffirmed anointing of the sick as being *specially appropriate* for those near death, with the priest as the *ordinary* (normal) minister, thereby leaving the door ajar to later developments.

The twentieth century has seen this door opened wide, with a broad revival of the ministry of healing. The Anglican Prayer Book of 1928 re-introduced anointing for healing (but not last rites). Vatican II provided for anointing (on head and hands) as restoring people to health of body, mind and/or spirit. A Maundy Thursday liturgy was introduced for the blessing of the three oils: the oil for admission to the catechumenate, also used in exorcisms, the chrism for confirmation, and ordinary olive oil for healing. This clarified the various uses of oil and reaffirmed the ministry of healing. Meanwhile, some charismatic and other traditions have discovered the value of oil in healing, and some argue for rediscovering the power of essential oils. Some would sharply dissent from this, but we have noted that sacraments always build on the inherent properties of matter.[3]

In the same period the ministry of exorcism or deliverance has revived, though in two markedly different contexts. One is the very public and dramatic healing and exorcism that are focal to worship in many charismatic churches. Here the focus is on the healer himself (very rarely 'herself') who is felt to have been anointed by the Spirit with special powers. The other is the much more sacramental exorcism now provided in the revived catechumenate, and via the appointment of official 'exorcists' who generally act in a very restrained and cautious way, genuine demon possession being regarded as rare, with psychological explanations taking priority.

Healing and Deliverance in the Age of Scientific Medicine

What are we to make of the sacrament of healing, and possibly exorcism, in an age where most people understand sickness in terms of medical complaints, germ-borne diseases and psychological complexes? Jesus' world, where healing and deliverance could be seen as part of a cosmic struggle with dark powers, has vanished. So, has the ministry of healing lost its sacramental sign value, and degenerated into an outdated superstition? I list here some possible views, adapting Niebuhr's typology (see Chapter 7).

- *Christ against medicine* Evil is real; modern medicine is jargon. Modern psychology was devised by atheists and is no more to be trusted than Ouija boards. We should avoid modern medicine and trust in the methods Jesus used. A strong 'pre-modern' approach, held by the Christian Scientists.
- *Christ of medicine* Demons and faith healing are superstitions. There is no evidence that prayer makes any difference. Rational people will rely on modern medicine and psychology, which is where Christ is to be seen at work today. A strong 'modern' approach.
- *Christ in the margins of medicine* 'Demons of the gaps': where medicine fails, pray and anoint; where psychotherapy fails, exorcise. Some diocesan exorcists actually work on this basis, exorcizing only when no psychological problem can be identified, when on another view it would be precisely the psychologically damaged that might need exorcism! Like the 'God of the gaps', this is an arguably rather weak response to the challenges of modernism.
- *Christ and medicine in paradox* Demons and complexes are different ways of talking about the same thing. The human body and mind are mysteries into which medicine and theology each provide their partial insight. Medical cure and anointing with prayer approach the same problem in paradoxically different, but ultimately complementary ways. Other approaches – alternative medicines and therapies – may provide other insights that work. A 'post-modern' approach: we just have to be pragmatic rather than dogmatic, and use what works best.
- *Christ above medicine* Sacramental healing and deliverance do for the soul what medicine does for our physical parts and psychology for the mind. They work on different levels. Ultimately it is the healing of the soul that matters, and this can triumph over chronic medical conditions and even death itself. But medicine and psychology can be of assistance on their subordinate level.
- *Christ the transformer of medicine* Here I take the cue from Yoder (1994) and Wink (1992), who identify the demons and powers with socio-political

forces which dominate humans and prevent their flourishing. Medicine and therapy typically address the individual and seek personal cure. But many of our ailments and our complexes stem from social conditions in the families and societies in which we grow and live. So perhaps (and this is my suggestion now) the ministries of healing and deliverance serve to set medicine in the context of that wider struggle with the powers. Medicine is not rejected, but transformed, by being seen not only in terms of achievable individual goals, but as part of a greater social and even cosmic struggle for wholeness, which is never over but which Christ fills with constantly renewed hope. So Wink describes prayer as 'rattling on God's cage' to rouse him to fight with us against the oppressing powers.

Discussion

Discuss the above views. What is your own?
What differences do you see, if any, between western society's approach to suffering, expressed in the healthcare system, and that of the church, expressed in the sacrament of healing?

Sacraments and the Whole Living Organism

We have just described the sacrament of healing as restoring the person to a wholeness of life, but what do we mean by this wholeness, which is personal but also social and even cosmic? Here I pause to suggest ways in which the sacraments, because of their cosmic dimension, touch the human being at the most basic level in which we participate as organisms in the life of the cosmos.

- *Baptism* relates to our 'natality',[4] our status as *born* beings. We are alive, but the process of life is full of the chaos which water symbolizes; in fact we are 90 per cent water! We need to wash and eliminate waste, processes which water also signifies.
- *Confirmation* – particularly in the form of chrismation where the senses are sealed with fragrant oil – relates to our status as *sensing* organisms, and through the senses, *learning*, intellectual organisms. In a world full

of beauty but also much junk – junk food, junk sex in the form of pornography, and junk commodities – our senses need a repeated purification and sealing so that our minds may be fixed on the good and the true.

- The *eucharist* obviously relates to our status as *feeding* beings, who live by eating and drinking. Probably our first awareness of an outside world is through our drinking of our mother's milk. Medieval writers like Anselm and Mother Julian write of the eucharist as a suckling at the breast of our 'mother' Christ. It is a wonderful mystery that the Christian God is believed to come to his people in this most basic of ways.

- *Reconciliation* relates to our status as naturally *fighting*, aggressive, competitive beings, qualities not evil in themselves, but meaning that we need to be reconciled and brought to peace if kingdom values are to prevail.

- *Healing* relates to our status as *growing, but wounded and mortal* beings, vulnerable to diseases of body and mind and destructive complexes and addictions, the things once called 'demons'. Our minds and bodies have the capacity to grow and heal, but need assistance from medicine and the sacraments. And in the end we do not heal, but die; nevertheless the sacrament of healing consecrates this dying to an ultimate healing or salvation.

- *Ordination* relates to our status as *working, creative* beings, needing a vocation in life, however humble, in order to prosper and gain a sense of worth. Luther was surely right to stress this universality of Christian vocation. Ordination obviously relates to a specific vocation, which includes the vocation to guide all Christians in their vocation (see next chapter).

- *Marriage* relates to our status as *sexual, procreative* beings, made for tenderness, desire, love and joy. Not all are called to marriage, and among the married not all have children, but the married couple delighting in the nurture of their children perhaps symbolizes the joyous, embodied and creative quality of good friendship and partnership for people of all circumstances and sexualities.

Discussion

Discuss the above. Are all aspects of human life covered by these sacraments; are some missing; and can the wholeness of human life be achieved by just two sacraments?

Figure 10. Dimensions of Healing.

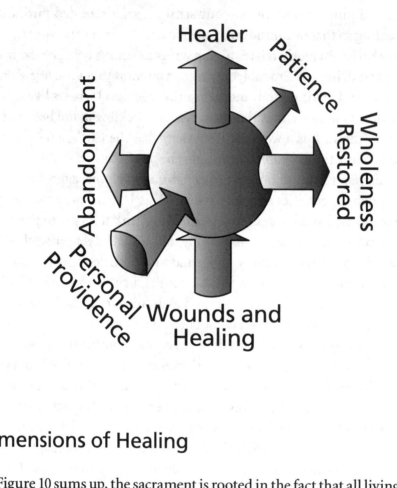

Dimensions of Healing

As Figure 10 sums up, the sacrament is rooted in the fact that all living things can experience damage and wounds, and all have the power to heal; medicine enhances these powers, while sacramental healing uses touch and salving oil to link them to Christ, who in his healing and his mortal wounding on the cross, did final battle with the powers that harm. Spiritually the sacrament relates to the times when we feel abandoned to spiritual and physical pains we can do nothing about, and ultimately to death. But whether we live or die it restores us to wholeness in the communion of saints. We remember the tender mercy God has shown in history to the afflicted, and learn 'the stature of waiting' (cf. Vanstone, 2004) for the coming of the kingdom.

Further Reading

Bernhard Poschmann, 1964, *Penance and the Anointing of the Sick*, New York: Herder and Herder.

Reconciliation

The American Book of Common Prayer, 1977, New York: The Seabury Press.

Dietrich Bonhoeffer, 1954, *Life Together*, New York: Harper and Row; and London: SCM Press.

John Chryssavagis, 1990, *Repentance and Confession in the Orthodox Church*, Brookline: Holy Cross Orthodox Press.

Hugh Connolly, 1995, *The Irish Penitentials*, Kells and Derry: Four Courts Press.

Tad Guzie and John McIlhon, 1979, *The Forgveness of Sin*, Sydney: St Thomas More Press.

F. J. Heggen, 1967, *Confession and the Service of Penance*, London and Melbourne: Sheed and Ward.

Theodore Jennings, 1988, *The Liturgy of Liberation*, Nashville: Abingdon Press.

Joseph Martos, 2001, *Doors to the Sacred*, Ligouri, Missouri: Ligouri/Triumph.

C. F. D. Moule, 1998, *Forgiveness and Reconciliation and other New Testament Themes*, London: SPCK.

Kenan Osbourne, 1990, *Reconciliation and Justification*, Mahwah and New York: Paulist Press.

Robert Schreiter, 1992, *Reconciliation: Mission and ministry in a changing social order*, London: Orbis.

Peter Sedgwick (ed.), 2004, *Rethinking Sentencing: A contribution to the debate*, London: Church House Publishing.

Max Thurian, 1958, *Confession*, London: SCM Press.

Anointing for Healing

Diocese of Bristol: Bishop's Advisory Group on the Church's Ministry of Healing. *Gifts of Healings*, available at http://bristol.anglican.org/gifts_of_healing/gifts_of_healing.htm

Michael Dudley and Geoffrey Rowell, 1993, *The Oil of Gladness*, Collegeville, Minnesota: The Liturgical Press.

James Empereur, 1982, *Prophetic Anointing: God's call to the sick, the elderly and the dying*, Wilmington: Michael Glazier.

Morton Kelsey, 1995, *Healing and Christianity*, Minneapolis: Augsburg Fortress Press.

James Lapsley, 1972, *Salvation and Health*, London: Westminster Press.

Denis and Matthew Linn, 1978, *Healing Life's Hurts*, Mahwah and New York: Paulist Press.

Morris Maddocks, 1990, *The Christian Healing Ministry*, London: SPCK.

Michael Perry (ed.), 1996, *Deliverance: Psychic disturbances and occult involvement*, London: SPCK.

John Sanford, 1992, *Healing Body and Soul*, Westminster: John Knox.

Linda Smith, 2003, *Healing Oils, Healing Hands*, Armada: HTSM.

W. H. Vanstone, 2004, *The Stature of Waiting*, London: Darton, Longman and Todd.

Walter Wink, 1992, *Engaging the Powers*, Minneapolis: Augsburg Fortress Press.

John Howard Yoder, 1994, *The Politics of Jesus*, Grand Rapids: Eerdmans.

12

Symbols of Vocation: Ordination and Marriage

In this chapter we consider the two sacraments by which sacraments perpetuate themselves: marriage, which enables new people to be created, without whom there would be no sacraments; and ordination, which creates new ministers of the sacraments.

Prophets of the Sacrament

Through most of its history the church has allowed most of the sacraments to be administered only by those ordained to do so. The main exceptions have been baptism, which a layperson can administer in urgent circumstances; anointing for healing, in some periods; and marriage, which on one view the couple administer to each other. In episcopal churches confirmation (in the West until recent changes) and ordination have required a bishop, while the eucharist and reconciliation require a priest. Nevertheless, the minister is not normally the most significant person involved. In the eucharist the whole community or a large part of it receive the sacrament, but in all the others the recipient is a specific person or group of people. In these sacraments, the minister merely produces the sign; it is the baptized, confirmed, reconciled, anointed, ordained and married who are called to bear in their lives the fruit of the sacrament, the reality it signifies. Béguerie and Duchesneau (1980,

p. 76) call them the 'prophets of the sacrament', because in their transformed lives they 'announce the living word of God'.

With that crucial point in mind, we consider ordination, a sacrament whose fruit is people who will minister the sacraments of which others will be the prophets, others will bear the fruit.

Prototypes of Ordained Ministry

Ministers pre-date Christianity, of course: shamans, magicians, priests, monks, nuns, rabbis, imams and holy men and women of various kinds have held roles of varying degrees of closeness to that of the Christian ordained minister.

> ## Exercise
>
> Consider the above titles. List the main roles associated with those who bear them (many will overlap). Which do you think are appropriate to a Christian minister?

In the Hebrew Bible we hear of several categories important to us:

• *The priesthood* A hereditary institution based on the temple, whose main business was the administration of the law. This included the offering of worship and sacrifice, but also many duties we would regard as 'secular'.
• *Prophets* A much looser group (though some of the prophets may have also been priests or at least have been closely linked to temple worship), called by God and often given visions and verbal messages. They seem to have stood apart from institutions and carried great authority to speak words of judgement even to kings.
• *Sages* A much later and even looser group of people who reflected on God's ways in the universe in the writings described as Wisdom literature.

All of these concepts have been applied to the ministry of Jesus. He was not a hereditary priest, but was regarded in Hebrews as the one true Priest; not a trained rabbi, but many discern enigmatic sage-like wisdom as the core of his teaching; while others emphasize his kinship to the prophets, with his authoritative end-time message, accompanied by mysterious signs. Recent scholars have adopted the rhyme (alleged to go to the rhythm of 'rich man, poor man...') concerning the various roles that have been discerned in Jesus: 'Wandering preacher, zealot, activist, magician/Cynic peasant, prophet, wisdom-logician'.

From Jesus to the Catholic Pattern

The route from this many faceted ministry of Jesus to the ordained ministry is tortuous. For some traditions, as we shall see, underlying continuity is vital. But it cannot be historically proven, and must remain a matter of faith. The story runs something like this (see Figure 11) (cf. Melinsky, 1992):

1 It is clear that Jesus called twelve disciples, with Peter as their leader (Matt. 16.13–23), sending them on a mission of healing and teaching to the people of Israel (Matt. 10.1–14) and in the end, to all the nations (Matt. 28.16–end). They loom large in the Acts of the Apostles, but their symbolic role, relating to the twelve tribes of the new Israel, was specific to the Jewish context, and the Twelve as leaders were gradually eclipsed.

2 In terms of mission to the Gentiles, Paul soon became the undoubted leader. He regarded himself as an apostle, but his credentials were very different. Meanwhile the administration of the Judean church appears to have been taken over by James the brother of Jesus. Two distinct styles of ministry now prevailed. In the Pauline mission, charismatic ministries proliferated. Paul used the analogy of the body that requires every member as an analogy for the way everyone has a spirit-initiated ministry in the body of Christ (1 Cor. 12). Some degree of hierarchical order seems to be implied in this, however, as the Spirit gives the church 'first apostles, second prophets, third teachers; then deeds of power, then gifts of healing, forms of assistance, forms of leadership, various kinds of tongues' (1 Cor. 12.28). Meanwhile an administration of elders (presbyters) and deacons, close to the leadership of the Jewish synagogue, predominated in the Judean church.

Figure 11. From Jesus to the Catholic Ministry.

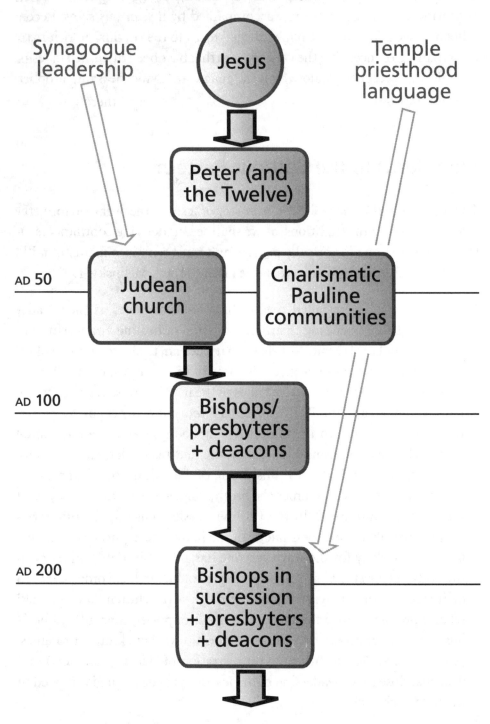

3 Despite the decline of the Judean church, by the end of the New Testament period, the pastoral epistles (Timothy and Titus) describe the latter pattern prevailing. The result was a twofold ministry of people called either overseers (*episkopoi*, our 'bishops') or elders (*presbyteroi*), responsible for the teaching; and deacons (public servants or ministers) responsible for practical matters like the distribution of charity (though there are various understandings of their role).

4 By the third century the former role was split between the bishops, who oversaw cities and their surrounding territories, and presbyters, who deputized for them in individual congregations. The bishops began to derive their authority from Jesus via an 'apostolic succession', not at this stage a succession of ordinations, but a succession of bishops of the same see. Thus the bishops of Rome derived their authority from Peter and Paul, who were martyred in that city.

5 At this period the language of sacred, sacrificing priesthood (*hiereus* in Greek, *sacerdos* in Latin) began to be applied to the bishops, first by Cyprian (c. 200–58). This was later extended to the presbyters. Our word 'priest' derives from '*presbyter*', but has connotations of sacrificing officiant as well as elder.

6 Finally a 'sacrament' of ordination was taken over from the secular rite whereby someone ascended to a higher 'order' in society. The robes that set these higher orders apart, notably the scarf or 'stole', the mark of a higher official, were adopted as a mark of the ordained.

All the elements of the Catholic understanding of ordination to the threefold ministry were now present, and would remain the foundation of Orthodox and western Catholic understandings. Ordination on this understanding confers authority both to preach the word of God and to consecrate and offer the sacramental body of Christ. The apostolic succession formed the backbone that held the church together and ensured sound doctrine. But the developing church hierarchy also helped hold wider society together, as priests through their learning gained a role in the state as civil servants or clerks – whence the term 'clergy' – while bishops became powerful prelates and the monastic orders became the place where classical culture – albeit selectively – was preserved and developed.

In the West, celibacy became regarded as essential to priesthood. The bishop of Rome gained increasing authority, until communion with the see of Rome was seen as defining the bounds of the church, and finally Vatican I (1868–70) vested the infallibility of the church in its spokesman the pope. In Vatican II it was acknowledged that God's grace could work outside of the church and, through baptism, make genuine Christians, but in the absence of genuine ordinations, there could be no real church other than the Roman. The Eastern Orthodox resisted these developments, and regard the church as a confederation of equal national churches, with ultimate authority vested in the ecumenical councils, not in any individual.

Priests or Ministers?

The Protestant Reformation rejected the notion of the priest as a sacramental mediator. It was the whole church, for Luther, that was priestly in the *hiereus* sense. Christ was seen as passing his authority on via the disciples to the whole people of God, and it was by their authority and call the minister exercised his, not vice versa. The leaders of the people – in Luther's time, the monarchs of the realm – therefore, under God had ultimate authority over the church; the pope had none.

However, Calvin and the Puritans paved a way for revolution and democracy by asserting the right of congregations to depose ungodly governors, a right that was exercised in the execution of Charles I in the English Civil War. Calvin strove for a New Testament model of ministry, but this proved incapable of producing anything systematic.

The Church of England (along with the Swedish and Finnish Lutheran churches) retained bishops, the apostolic succession and the threefold ministry, thus combining Catholic ministry with a broadly reformed theology, features that have always been in tension. The mainstream Anglican view, however, is that this pattern of ministry is not of the *esse*, the essential being, of the church, but part of its *bene esse*, something that makes for well-being; and this has rendered reconciliation possible not only with the Episcopal churches just mentioned, in the recent Porvoo agreement, but also potentially with the Methodists and other non-episcopal churches. For the

Methodists, correspondingly, not having bishops is not necessarily regarded as of the *esse*; in fact many Methodist churches have retained them, and Wesley would have preferred to have had episcopally ordained ministers, but the English bishops refused to ordain them when needed for his mission in America.

The Anglicans retained the term 'priest' but tend to emphasize the pastoral rather than sacerdotal elements of priesthood, as beautifully summed up in this poem of the poet and priest George Herbert, which apply the description of the Aaronic priest's dress in Exodus 28.2–5 to the pastoral and spiritual work of a priest:

> Holinesse on the head,
> Light and perfections on the breast,
> Harmonious bells below, raising the dead
> To leade them unto life and rest.
> Thus are true Aarons drest.

The Main Disagreements

Many discussions are now going on to reconcile these different understandings (see Further Reading below). The main points of issue are:

- Whether ordination is a sacrament conferring an indelible character to the very *being* of the ordained, or whether it is a primarily a vocation, permanent or temporary, to *do* certain tasks. These views go by the proud name of 'ontological' and 'functional' respectively.
- Whether authority passes from Christ to the ordained via a separate apostolic succession, making ordained priesthood distinct from the royal priesthood of all the baptized; or whether it passes from him direct to all churches that rightly preach the word and administer the sacraments, so that ordained ministry belongs to and derives authority from the royal priesthood of all.
- What degree of continuity there might be between ordained ministry and the Old Testament priesthood.

- Whether the threefold ministry of bishops, priests and deacons is essential to the church, or desirable as part of its well-being, or not even desirable.
- Whether women should be ordained. Christ, the apostles and for nineteen centuries all the ordained were male, so the Catholic, Orthodox and some Protestant churches see the ordination of women as undermining the apostolic succession or the ability of the priest to represent Christ. Many Protestants reject the ideas of priesthood on which these arguments are based. Others argue that ordaining women is not breaking the succession or creating a new order of priest, simply extending the same ordination to people whose gender makes no difference to their capacity to represent Christ or do priestly work.

Discussion

Discuss your answers to these five questions.

Ordination rites are essentially similar, with variations, including readings, ordination vows before the bishop, singing of the hymn 'Come Holy Ghost', laying on of bishop's hands, dressing with stole (the scarf worn by priest or deacon), presentation of Bible, chalice and paten, sometimes anointing of the hands, celebration of the eucharist (with the new priests sometimes con-celebrating). The more Protestant churches reflect a different theology however in their emphasis on reception in the local church rather than a sacramental rite administered by a bishop.

There remains, however, a great deal that all churches would acknowledge as belonging to the minister. After distinguishing the ministry of the ordained from that of the apostles, BEM states in Article M11:

As heralds and ambassadors, ordained ministers are representatives of Jesus Christ to the community, and proclaim his message of reconciliation. As leaders and teachers they call the community to submit to the authority of Jesus Christ, the teacher and prophet, in whom law and prophets were fulfilled. As pastors, under Jesus Christ the chief shepherd, they assemble and guide the dispersed people of God, in anticipation of the coming Kingdom.

So What Do We Ordain People For?

Here are some definitions of aspects of the work of the ordained which have been offered. Some are traditional, others adaptations to modern times.

- *Administrator* Ensuring the church runs smoothly so the people of God can exercise their gifts to the full.
- *Enabler* Recognizing and developing the gifts of others and giving them appropriate work.
- *Performance director* Allocating parts in the drama of salvation, and also ensuring the people co-operate in acting it out.
- *Prophet* Challenging on behalf of the poor the powers that oppress people, and calling people to repentance and life in the kingdom.
- *Sage* The learned and cultured master who 'brings out of his treasure what is new and what is old' (Matt. 13.52) so as to help people find new ethical insight.
- *Soul friend* A companion and spiritual guide helping people in and outside the church on their own spiritual journey.
- *Holy fool* Foolish in the eyes of the wise and sophisticated, because pointing the way to the scandalous and foolish wisdom of the cross (1 Cor. 1.25).
- *Pastor* The good shepherd, seeking out the lost and guiding them into the fold.
- *General practitioner* Holding 'surgeries', attending to people's problems, helping in a general way, and referring to more specialist helpers where necessary.
- *Parson* A word that means simply 'person'. Someone 'on holiday in the parish', free to be herself and so show the way to fuller humanity.
- *Deacon* Serving the needs of others but, like a good butler, making suggestions as to the best spiritual wine. (A *diakonos* was more of a butler or public servant than a menial *doulos* or slave.)
- *Suffering servant* Bearing the pains and sins of the people in a Christ-like way so as to bring them to his salvation.
- *Subversive* Infiltrating secular organizations and slipping in the subversive gospel message in a covert way. Contrasts with the overt confrontational stance of the prophet.

- *Liturgist* Maintaining the worship as the parish's 'response of being to the love of God' (Vanstone, 1977) – the one thing that cannot happen without the church.
- *Walking sacrament* A high-profile presence in the parish, as a sign of the kingdom, helping people become aware of and respond to the presence of God in their midst.

Exercise

Score the above on your own, then discuss in groups, then feed back, according to this scale.

2　Central to the calling of the minister
1　Important part of the calling
0　Something to bear in mind in ministry
-1　Not part of the minister's vocation
-2　Really bad idea, to be rejected wholeheartedly

Dimensions of Ordination

See Figure 12. Ordination is rooted in our need to be creative in the image of our creator; ordination serves to relate this priesthood of humanity and of the baptized to Christ, the ascended high priest, who calls us and sends us all as ministers of his kingdom. For this to happen we need people with an overall vision for the kingdom and how the gifts of the people can work together towards it; Moses and the prophets are the archetype here, calling the people through word and sacrament to freedom and away from the human tendency to settle for a diminishing life of servitude and idolatry.

The three dimensions also suggest the qualities needed in an ordained minister. He or she will need to be:

- Rooted in *tradition*, not slavishly but with a lively love of the creation, the word and the sacraments she is to share with others, as well as her own tradition.

Figure 12. Dimensions of Ordination.

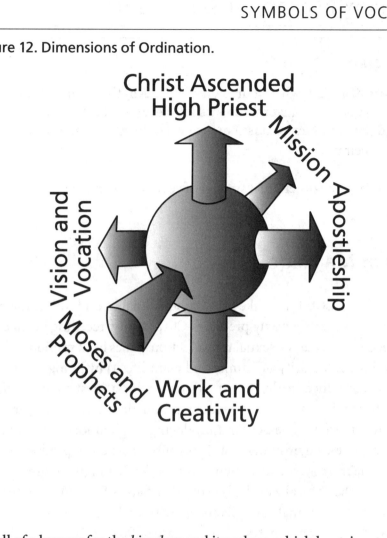

- Full of a hunger for the *kingdom* and its values, which he strives to see fulfilled in society more widely than just in the church.
- A committed but by no means uncritical participant in the life of the *church*, able to develop others in their roles and work convivially within it.
- A person of deep *spirituality*, prayer and self-understanding, well accompanied by her own soul friend, and able to accompany others on their journey.
- Down to *earth*, humble, and at ease with her own humanity, sexuality and embodiment, and so able to make room in her life for others.
- A loving follower of *Christ*, committed to shaping the life of the church on the model of his life through word and sacrament.

Exercise

Compare this list with your own ideals. Anything to criticize or add? Look at some advertisements for clergy posts. How far do the job and person descriptions compare with these ideals?

Now we turn to the other great symbol of vocation, marriage.

Roots of Marriage

Marriage as an institution – like priesthood, arguably, and unlike the other sacraments – obviously vastly pre-dates Christianity, receding beyond historical memory. Its basis – sexual reproduction – goes back millions of years and includes the majority of animal and plant life. Why living things have evolved to reproduce in this way is something of a mystery in itself, but probably has to do with the way sexual reproduction shuffles the genes, increasing resistance to diseases, and producing original forms, so speeding adaptation to new environments. It is because of sexual reproduction that each of us (apart from identical twins) is genetically unique. A great deal of the beauty of the natural world has evolved because of sexual reproduction, which means that animals and plants vie with each other, in form, colour and behaviour, to secure mates (or in the case of flowers, bees and other insects) to reproduce. Sexual reproduction thus accounts for the oldest of rites, courtship rituals, though of course these do not have all the features we have ascribed to ritual!

In the Hebrew Bible, God creates beings male and female from the start, and commands them all to be fruitful and multiply (Gen. 1). With human gender there is a difference, however. Human males and females are in God's image (vv. 26–27). The conclusion need not be drawn, as it sometimes is, that male and female need to come together in marriage to form the image of God; the passage is probably simply affirming, against patriarchal tendencies, that women are as much in the image of God as men (cf. Vorgrimler,

1992, p. 286). Again, in Genesis 2, the woman is initially created not for reproduction, but for companionship and support, because 'it is not good that the man should be alone' (v. 18). So from the first, human gender is related to companionship. This theological point has a biological confirmation: John Macquarrie notes (1997, p. 218) that in the human animal, sex most often takes place face to face, and is not limited to the cycles of reproduction, thus making it a personal act. One might add that the nakedness of the human means that sexual embrace arouses the whole being, not just areas related to reproduction.

Later in the Bible, however, the reproductive side is reasserted, in the blessings with which God promises abundant descendants to Abraham, 'as the stars of heaven and as the sand upon the seashore' (Gen. 22.17). So patriarchal marriage served to secure descendants. The patriarchs often had several wives, while adultery bore the death penalty, probably because it meant a man could not be sure who his descendants were. Nevertheless this reproductive basis was enriched with companionship, and in the Song of Songs especially, erotic love was valued in itself, as a source of joy.

Foundations of Christian Marriage

Christianity arose in a starker perspective: the coming kingdom seemed to make marriage and procreation redundant. Jesus acknowledged those who 'have made themselves eunuchs for the sake of the kingdom' (Matt. 19.12), and taught that there was no marriage in heaven, because we would resemble the angels (presumably in their transcendence of gender or sex: Matt. 22.30; Mark 12.25; Luke 20.34). Sex never became for Christianity, as it did for Islam, one of the delights of heaven. St Paul urged that celibacy was the best option, but it was 'better to marry than to be aflame with passion' (1 Cor. 7.9). Such trends bore fruit, later, in the monastic movements.

Meanwhile earthly marriage was seen as a sign. St Paul correlated the relation between man and wife to the 'mystery' of Christ in relation to his bride the church, an image picked up in the great marriage of the Lamb with his celestial bride, consummating the whole of history, in Revelation 19. Such images, along with Christ's presence at the wedding at Cana (John 2.1–11 – a miracle with no purpose other than increasing joy) were seen as justifying the joys of marriage as a sacrament expressing the deep love of Christ in a relationship of love and procreation. The erotic language of the Song of Songs was applied by the celibate to the mystic journey, but via a roundabout route Christianity, having cast suspicions on both sex and patriarchal marriage, began to develop its own sacramental concept of marriage as a loving union between man and woman in which the love between Christ and his church shines forth. This demanded, over against patriarchal conceptions where marriage was a contract between families, a focus on the voluntary contract between the man and woman, and on a connection between marriage and that peculiar state which combines the erotic and the mystical, known as 'being in love'.

So a sacrament that had its roots deep in human nature rather than specific revelation, nevertheless came to have a profound Christianizing effect on what human society does with human nature, creating patterns of romantic love and the love-based marriage which could not have been predicted from either Christian faith or human nature alone, but arose partly from the sacramental interaction of the two (cf. Lewis, 1977).

Discussion

Do you see romantic love and love-based marriage as universal to human nature or something Christianity has helped to foster?

Developing Theologies of Marriage

This was a very gradual process, however. Only with the conversion of the empire did marriage begin to become a Christian ceremony rather than a civil one, and the process was not completed until the twelfth century. Theologians were largely celibate, and resisted a sacrament based on such dubious 'matter' as sex. But in the West, following Augustine, it gradually became regarded as a sacrament imparting indelible character, so that divorce was viewed as impossible from the ninth century onwards. In the Orthodox Church, however, marriage after civil divorce is permitted up to seven times, and the Protestant churches have tended also, reluctantly, to relax the prohibition.

Lombard was the first explicitly to regard marriage as a sacrament in the case of those who are baptized. Aquinas explained that the couple's life together – including sexual consummation – was the matter of the sacrament, and their words of consent the form. This made the couple the ministers of the sacrament, and Duns Scotus affirmed the stronger point that the couple are the officiants of their own wedding ceremony. Symbols like the joining of hands or the exchanging of rings were taken as subsidiary.

There is a tension here. On the one hand these theologians wanted to restrict the sacramental nature of the rite to the baptized, because this was always regarded as the first sacrament, the doorway to all the others. On the other hand the sign of the sacrament – the vows and the committed life together – can obviously be undertaken by those outside the Christian fold. The usual answer lies in the fact that only for the baptized does a committed life point to the union between Christ and his church. Non-Christians can have wonderful married lives, but they are not striving to embody that union, so their lives are not sacraments of the kingdom.

In Orthodox tradition a different understanding holds: the priest marries the couple by means of the nuptial blessing. The couple are then crowned as a sign of their restoration as images of Christ the King. The reformers, meanwhile, denied the sacramentality of marriage, but stressed its value relative to celibacy, hitherto regarded as the higher calling.

Duns Scotus was not alone in seeing marriage as a contract making the messy business of sex permissible for the purpose of procreation. The Anglican Book of Common Prayer follows the medieval three purposes of marriage, listing procreation as the first and companionship as the third, with the second being 'a remedy against sin, and to avoid fornication; that such persons as have not the gift of continency might marry, and keep themselves undefiled members of Christ's body', thus avoiding the 'incontinence of brute beasts'.

Recent rites affirm all three purposes more positively. The new Anglican rite speaks positively of sex, and integrates the purposes:

> The gift of marriage brings husband and wife together in the delight and tenderness of sexual union and joyful commitment to the end of their lives. It is given as the foundation of family life in which children are born and nurtured and in which each member of the family, in good times and in bad, may find strength, companionship and comfort, and grow to maturity in love.

In the 1950s Roman Catholics likewise worked towards a personal rather than reproduction centred view of marriage, but in the 1960s the traditional line was reaffirmed with the condemnation of contraception. Latterly the Catholic Church has condemned all the new reproductive technologies that enable couples to have children when 'natural' sexual union fails to produce them.

The pattern of the marriage rite is similar, consisting of betrothal (statement of intent to marry), readings, exchange of vows (joining right hands), blessing and exchange of rings, prayers and nuptial blessing. The rite may be held in the context of a eucharist; in the Catholic Church this (the nuptual mass) is the norm, while the Anglican *Common Worship* provides for a careful integration of marriage and eucharist.

Current Controversies

Three sets of issues are coming to dominate discussion, and even in the Anglican Church threaten schism, today:

1 Should there be provision for divorce? Protestant, Catholic and Orthodox churches have different answers. On the one hand, Christ's words against divorce (Mark 10.11; Luke 16.18, softened in Matt. 5.31 and 19.9) represent the only rigorist statement about sexual ethics he makes. And if marriage creates a sacramental bond, it seems indissoluble. On the other hand, a brutal or destructive marriage can hardly be an effective sign of the love between Christ and the church. Is there not an analogy here with euchar-

istic bread that has decayed, which once bore the divine presence, but can do so no longer? Christians would agree, at least, that divorce is always tragic, and that Christians must not place individual fulfilment above the real bonds of love that exist in a family. But tragedies happen.

2 Currently there is growing provision for civil recognition of gay partnerships. Should such partnerships be blessed in church? Proponents argue that marriage itself began as a blessing of a civil institution, and that sexual joy and companionship are now seen positively, and no longer as having to be linked to procreation to be redeemable. Opponents point to the 'male and female' dimension of marriage from Genesis onward, and the irreducible gender imagery of Christ the bridegroom and the church the bride. Some also argue on biblical or natural law grounds that homosexuality is inherently sinful, and as such cannot be blessed.

3 Current trends are towards a phased approach to Christian commitment via RCIA and the like, people being encouraged to test the waters and proceed at their own pace. Should the commitment of marriage likewise be phased, celebrating engagement, cohabitation, birth of children and lifelong commitment separately? Proponents argue that the current rite is an amalgamation of what were once separate stages of betrothal and marriage, and that even devoutly Christian couples often do phase their commitment in this way, leading to dissonance between their lives and its sacramental expression (Guzie, 1981, pp. 89–91). Opponents would argue that the prohibition of sex outside marriage is non-negotiable, and a phased process would encourage sin and lead people away from salvation. Also, that couples might rest content with the lesser stages, rather than be led to that lifelong, sacramental commitment which the church believes, not unreasonably, to be the ideal context for the nurture of children, and the way to the total, unconditional sharing of one life between distinct persons in which the family, like a little 'domestic Church',[1] realizes among them the communion of the Trinity.

Discussion

Discuss your views on these issues.

Figure 13. Dimensions of Marriage.

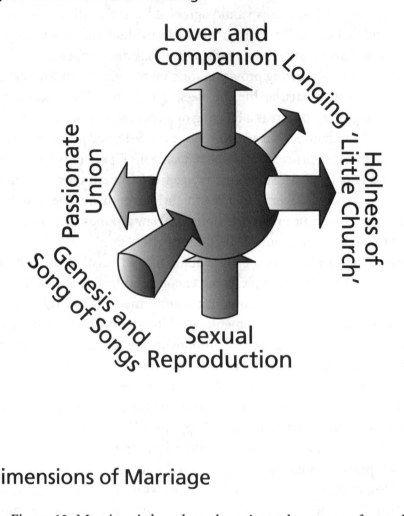

Dimensions of Marriage

See Figure 13. Marriage is based on the primeval mystery of sexual reproduction, which the church has used as an image of Christ's friendship and
love of us. Recalling the deepest origins of gender in Genesis and the eroti-
cism of the Song of Songs, mystics have made erotic love a symbol of our
union with God and our yearning (*epektasis* or reaching out in the darkness)[2] for the kingdom. But marriage reflects this spirituality back into the
human family, called to image the intimacy of the Trinity as a little church.
It is the only sacrament where the ministers and the 'prophets' (recipients)
are the same.

Further Reading

Ordination

P. Béguerie and C. Duchesneau, 1980, *How to Understand the Sacraments*, London: SCM Press.

Leonardo Boff, 1985, *Church, Charism, and Power*, London: SCM Press.

Council for Christian Unity of the General Synod of the Church of England: *The Porvoo Common Statement*, London: Church House; see www.porvoochurches. org/statements/en.htm.

Stephen Croft, 1999, *Ministry in Three Dimensions*, London: Darton, Longman and Todd.

C. Cruse, 1983, *New Testament Foundations of Ministry*, London: Marshall, Morgan and Scott.

J. T. Forestell, 1991, *As Ministers of Christ: The christological dimension of ministry in the New Testament*, Mahwah and New York: Paulist Press.

Robin Greenwood, 1994, *Transforming Priesthood*, London: SPCK.

George Guiver, 2001, *Priests in a People's Church*, London: SPCK.

Tad Guzie, 1981, *The Book of Sacramental Basics*, Mahwah and New York: Paulist Press.

A. B. Lawson, 1963, *John Wesley and the Christian Ministry*, London: SPCK.

John Macquarrrie, 1997, *A Guide to the Sacraments*, London: SCM Press.

Kenneth Mason, 1992, *Priesthood and Society*, Norwich: Canterbury Press.

M. A. H. Melinsky, 1992, *The Shape of the Ministry*, Norwich: Canterbury Press.

R. C. Moberly, 1969, *Ministerial Priesthood*, London: SPCK.

Alastair Redfern, 1999, *Ministry and Priesthood*, London: Darton, Longman and Todd.

Edward Schillebeeckx, 1997, *The Church with a Human Face*, London: SCM Press.

T. F. Torrance, 1955, *Royal Priesthood*, Edinburgh: Oliver and Boyd.

W. H. Vanstone, 1977, *Love's Endeavour, Love's Expense*, London: Darton, Longman and Todd.

Also see the ecumenical texts cited at the end of Chapter 6.

Marriage

Archbishop's Commission on the Christian Doctrine of Marriage, 1971, *Marriage, Divorce and the Church*, London: SPCK.

Paul Avis, 1989, *Eros and the Sacred*, London: SPCK.

Peter Brown, 1989, *The Body and Society: Men, women and sexual renunciation in early Christianity*, London: Faber and Faber.

Jack Dominian, 1983, *Marriage, Faith and Love*, London: Darton, Longman and Todd.

Peter J. Elliott, 1990, *What God Has Joined: The sacramentality of marriage*, Jedburgh: Alba.

C. S. Lewis, 1977, *The Allegory of Love*, Oxford: Oxford Paperbacks.

David and Vera Mace, 1986, *The Sacred Fire*, Nashville: Abingdon Press.

Philip Reynolds, 1994, *Marriage in the Western Church*, Boston: E. J. Brill.

Philip Sherrard, 1976, *Christianity and Eros*, London: SPCK.

Adrian Thatcher, 1999, *Marriage After Modernity: Christian marriage in postmodern times*, New York: University Press.

Adrian Thatcher, 2002, *Celebrating Christian Marriage*, London and New York: Continuum.

Max Thurian, 1959, *Marriage and Celibacy*, London: SCM Press.

Herbert Vorgrimler, 1992, *Sacramental Theology*, Collegeville, Minnesota: The Liturgical Press.

Christopher Webber, 1994, *Re-Inventing Marriage*, Milwaukee: Morehouse.

John Witte, 1997, *From Sacrament to Contract*, Westminster: John Knox.

Conclusion:
The Sacramental Prism

Throughout this book we have noted how sacraments have been seen as grounds of terrible divisions. Many Christians have been martyred for their views on the eucharist or the priesthood. But looking back, and thinking in terms of our three dimensions, it is possible to see history rather as presenting us with a prism, in which different aspects of the sacraments have been reflected back at different times. In this section I hope briefly to contemplate the prism as a whole. However, while a prism radiates the white light into seven colours, people have often numbered differently the sacramental colours that refract the pure light of God. I will consider first the case for having more than seven.

Other Possible Sacraments

We noted that for Augustine and the Fathers many things other than the seven were regarded as sacraments, in a world that was charged with the energies of God and sacramental of him. It remains to list a few rites that are almost sacraments, but the list is non-definitive:

- *Icons* The Orthodox believe that the veneration (not worship) of icons is essential to the liturgy. They have all the dimensions of sacraments. They represent a past revelation, but reach out to the final transfiguration when we shall see Christ in all things. They depict the individual 'icon' or image of God in the human person, but in a manner that gathers the believer into the communion of saints as he worships surrounded by their images. They are very ordinary, portable wood, yet depict in subtle stylized ways the Mystery of Christ. In themselves they are not rites, but the veneration of icons by the Orthodox – lighting candles, kissing, contemplating, bowing or prostrating – might well be regarded as sacramental.

- *Scriptures or Preaching* are widely regarded as effective, grace-bearing en-counters with the Word of God. The Orthodox sometimes describe the scriptures as the 'verbal icon of Christ'. The administration of the sacra-ments is always accompanied by scriptural readings; but to preserve the notion of a completeness of 'word and sacrament' together, it might seem preferable not to conflate the two by treating the readings as sacramental in themselves.

- *Laying on of hands for the Gift of the Spirit* The charismatic movement, following some trends in the early church, believe in a 'baptism of the Spirit' as an experience independent of water baptism, enabled by prayer and laying on of hands. The theology is a little like that of chrismation or confirmation, but the practice is more spontaneous and related to per-sonal decision and desire. As an outward sign of an inner grace this action is clearly sacramental, though it is not clear whether all the dimensions of a sacrament are present. The individual seems to override the corporate, and the historical rooting is not very clear.

- *Washing of Feet* was given a quasi-baptismal interpretation of commit-ment and cleansing by Christ. It is part of the Lord's supper in the Church of God of Prophecy, and part of the Maundy Thursday celebrations in the western Catholic tradition. Historically rooted and instituted (John 13.14–15) and a vivid image of the love of the kingdom, deeply personal yet corporate, using the literally 'earthy' symbolism of feet to present the mystery of Christ, it is surely sacramental in these contexts.

- *Speaking in Foreign Tongues (glossolalia)* is recorded in several cultures. For Christians it was initiated at Pentecost (Acts 2.1–13). Paul described it, emphasizing the need for orderliness and interpretation so that the tongues could build up the church. Those who have experienced this speak of an inner liberation to praise God on a level that is deeper than understanding. In Acts 2 it seems to symbolize the restored unity of all humankind, as people become able to understand one another's language. Something very physical and bodily is here connected with the deep mystery of Christ and the Spirit; a personal sense of freedom is (ideally) balanced by a corporate concern for edification; there are clear historical roots combined with a global, eschatological significance of human unity in Christ. All of this makes for a potentially very rich sacrament. On the other hand, this phenomenon has no minister, only a 'prophet'.

Discussion

Are there any of these you would like to see as more, or less, part of regular church life?

Seven Sacraments in Three Dimensions

Given this possibility of extending the number of the sacraments, plus the fact that many churches speak only of two, is there anything to be gained by focusing on the Catholic seven? I suggest there are two main reasons.

One is paradoxically ecumenical – that all the churches practise some form of all seven, the dispute only being whether the term 'sacrament' should be used. Healing may be present only in a loose sense in which all churches prioritize pastoral care for the sick, confirmation only as the decision made at believer's baptism, or as a pastoral opportunity to reaffirm baptismal faith. Repentance may be expressed via an altar call rather than private confession. But clearly there is a felt need for these opportunities to be present in all churches. Even the Quakers, who prefer the white light of silence to sacramental practices, find in this silence the renewal, nurture, fellowship, peace, healing, vocation and love of Christ. But the 'sacraments' just suggested – icons, washing of feet, tongues, etc. – are not ecumenical; they exist only in some denominations.

The other reason moves on from this to a bolder suggestion that might be made – that the churches do not just happen to have these signs and rites in common, but that they are the signs and rites they need to have if they are to

Table 4. Seven Sacraments in Three Dimensions.

	History	Kingdom Value (see p. 78)	Church (see p. 165)	Spirituality (see p. 104)	Cosmos (see p. 194)	Christ
Baptism	Red Sea . . .	Humble joy; eternal life	'Catholic' (universal) belonging by grace	Conversion, spiritual rebirth, repentance	Water: chaos creation and birth	His baptism: death and resurrection
Confirmation	Kings: David anointed Messiah	Education, encouragement	Active 'apostolic' membership	Way of affirmation and illumination	Chrism: senses	Calling and teaching
Eucharist	Passover Lamb, freedom in promised land	Sacrificial sharing	'Holy' koinonia	Way of union with God	Bread, wine: feeding	Table fellowship, Last supper, resurrection
Reconciliation	Exile and return	Justice and peace	Restoration of 'unity', peace-making church	Way of purgation, renunciation, 'active night' of St John of the Cross	Conflict and resolution	Forgiving, befriending outcasts, bearing sins
Healing	Personal providence: God of the patriarchs	Patience, 'stature of waiting', therapy	Restoration of 'holiness' in sense of wholeness	Way of negation, unchosen pains, 'passive night' of St John of the Cross	Salving oil, wounds and healing	Wounded healer, confronting the powers that harm

Ordination	Moses the lawgiver, prophets' calling	Mission to welcome kingdom on earth	Ensuring 'apostolic' continuity of life and teaching	Vocation and vision, way of creativity	Work, creativity	Ascension as high priest, sending Spirit
Marriage	Genesis, Song of Songs	Family life, little kingdom	Embodiment of unity in family as 'little church'	Way of union, reaching out to God in love alone	Sexuality, propagation	Loving companion

minister a complete salvation, ministering the whole Christ to make a whole people. That is, they are the effective signs that are, together, necessary for the people's salvation (though not all of them are necessary to each person's salvation, and not all need to be officially regarded as sacraments).

The completeness is suggested by Table 4, which summarizes what we have learnt in this book. But we need to qualify this completeness in two ways.

The Whole Christ for the Whole Person

The first qualification lies in what sacraments cannot of themselves do. Even if we believe that the sacramental reality is accomplished assuredly by God working through these signs *ex opere operato*, that does not mean sacraments can mechanically effect salvation irrespective of how we use them in our lives. The 'reality' of the sacrament, the divine grace in its many aspects here listed, requires that we use it wisely in the context of a responsible life-journey that is serious about opening our lives to Christ through them. Conversely we do not need to accept the now discarded teaching that divine grace can operate *only* through the sacramental system of the church.

But sacraments do open the opportunity of abundant life. They make possible – the Table tries to show – the giving of the whole Christ, the goal and perfection of the whole cosmos, to the whole person in a whole society, in the context of the whole past, opening up a future in which all shall be made whole.

The Mystery in New Translations?

But finally, how can this possibility be realized now, in our age? This brings us to our second qualification. It is important that we do not think of the sacramental system as we have it now as fixed for all time. Christ is our light, but the prism of the age has in the past, and can in the future, divide his colours in more ways than one. In discussing the relation of the seven mysteries to the Mystery of Christ (see Chapter 5), I suggested that the sacramental system that has evolved to what we have now represents a kind of 'translation' that captures the gist of what Christ by his life and teaching instituted for us. As the church has translated this, however, it has placed sometimes undue stress on itself as the mediator of tradition. It has tended to 'ecclesialize' or 'churchify' what after all was initially table friendship and splashing in rivers. The church has seen itself as containing the sacraments, such that one can only increase the sacramental reach of Christ through making more people belong to the church. But in Western Europe the membership trends of all voluntary organizations is downward, and while we must not despair of growing the church again, perhaps growth can only come through allowing the rays of sacramental colour to penetrate more deeply into the world around us than the sharpening boundaries of the church currently let them.

In the previous century it is precisely the 'non-churchy' dimensions that have been re-emphasized, as the sacraments have been seen to relate to the whole organism and the whole cosmos; to be pointers and expressions of a spiritual journey that, thanks to them, can become less lonely, more shared, as on the catechumenate path; and to embody the values of the kingdom in a way that challenges the whole way we in our age misvalue the world and each other.

Perhaps the task of this century is to bring our church and missionary practice in line with these new insights, so that we can release the sacraments from their 'Babylonish captivity' to be transformers of society and the earth. Quite what this might mean it is too early in the day to be clear about, for it involves tasks – such as a working out of how a society might embody in its institutions a sacramental approach to crime, justice and restoration; and how institutional power can be exercised 'for the healing of the peoples' rather than the preservation of the institution – which despite its twenty-century history the church has scarcely begun to address. But because they are both signs of the kingdom and social practices, sacraments have more chance of providing part of the answer to these social questions than the current tendency to try to save the world by papal condemnation or synod motion. For me, the Greenbelt Festival shows one place where answers are beginning to happen – a throng of people of all ages, genders, sexualities and races, pulsing with signs and discourses and dramas and songs that lead the way to something that feels a bit like a new translation of the life of Christ into our age. But there are many other places where the same thing is happening in different ways, and the reader may be aware of some.

Discussion

Discuss whether we need to celebrate Christ and/or the sacraments outside the church and de-churchify them; and if so, how you think this might be done or where to your knowledge it is being done.

We conclude with a poem that describes the sacraments as issuing from the wounded side of Christ, and how the church has guarded these mysteries as its own. But on the cross the old imprisoning powers have been defeated. We just need to learn to release the mysteries to sweep aside the old swords.

However high we climb, we return time
and again to our first fall: the moment buried
in childhood's tenderness, when the brutal chill of life
first ran us through.
                              So now the lance's rape recalls
the serpent and the tree: from trauma's opening,
                              new Eve is born, takes fruit
of blood and guards it, her own
                              private mystery.
And in this child we see
                              all the vengeful mercy,
passionate purity, virgin lust, caring
                              condemnation and jealous beauty
of the Bride, the everlasting Church.

                    The Patriarch here dies, and floods
the world with all he held; such mercy-tide
                              – could she but set it free –
might sweep aside old Roman swords,
                              and change our history.[1]

Appendix: The Jewish Festivals:

Table 5 fills in the answers for the Table 1 on page 22.

Table 5: Table of Jewish Festivals completed.

Rite	When does it happen?	What is used?	What is done?	What is remembered?	What is celebrated or achieved?
Passover	First Month March–April	Lamb, unleavened bread, bitter herbs	Slain, doorposts smeared, roast and eaten	Exodus from Egypt	Liberation
Pentecost	7 weeks later May	First-fruits of harvest	Offered	Wandering of patriarchs and exodus	Bounty of God
'Covenant'	(No time specified, maybe never actually done)	Bull, altar	Sacrifice, sprinkling altar and people with blood	Covenant between God and people	Eating and drinking with God
Sukkoth	7th month September	Fruit and boughs of trees	'Tents' built	Life in wilderness	(Sense of 'travelling light' with God?)
Yom Kippur	New Year Autumn	Goat (ram's horn)	Sent out into wilderness	God's appearance at mercy seat?	Cancelling of sins

Notes

Preface

1 'Objectivity and Religious Symbol'. I hope to make this available on my website, www.holydust.org.

Chapter 1

1 Durkheim (2001) and (in a different way) Douglas (2002, 2003) regard the sacred–profane distinction as fundamental to ritual and a basic means by which it structures individuals into society. The ritual dimension to myth is stressed by Eliade, Harrison and Hooke, while the magic or technological dimension – ritual as a way of relating to the physical environment – is the focus for Malinowski, Evans-Pritchard, Leach and Parsons. The notion of negative ritual – taboo – is widely accepted. On the whole these are differences of emphasis rather than opposed views.

Chapter 2

1 It was the philosopher Hume in the eighteenth century who defined, and opposed, miracles in this sense, though the view of sacraments and miracles as 'supernatural' goes back to the Middle Ages at least. The New Testament term, however, means simply 'marvel'.

Chapter 4

1 The term 'Fathers' denotes the theologians who came after New Testament times and leading into the 'Dark Ages', the so-called 'Patristic' period which shaped

the main lines of belief about Christ and the Trinity as expressed in the creeds. I apologize for the sexism, but – as feminists have been quick to point out – these theologians were in fact virtually all male. To speak of the 'Church Fathers and Mothers' would be both patronizing and misleading.

Chapter 5

1 For some of this section I am indebted to the excellent presentation of Schillebeeckx by Joseph Martos (2001) in *Doors of the Sacred*, pp. 110–12.
2 Though Calvin at least would say he retained the incarnational unity of divine and human; otherwise Christians could hardly say as they always have that Jesus is Lord, at the Father's right hand.
3 At least this is true of my own Church of England, where synods cannot agree whether we 'offer' bread to God and wine or 'set them before' him, though both concepts translate the same Greek term *prosphero*.
4 John Hick (1977) famously compared the doctrine that Jesus is human and divine to the idea of a 'square circle' (*The Myth of God Incarnate*, p. 178), but in a subsequent article Herbert McCabe pointed out the very error about levels which I am pointing to now.
5 For further discussion of levels and emergence, see my 1990, pp. 205ff, my website www.holydust.org, and my *Transfiguring God*, Chapter 4, available on that site.
6 Images of Christ and dove courtesy of http://royaltyfreeclipart.com.
7 The crucifix here is a remarkable one now in St Barnabas, Knowle West, Bristol. It was made from waste wood by a boy from the local secondary school, since closed.
8 Of course, our present legal systems fall lamentably short of this redemptive ideal; see Chapter 11 on reconciliation.

Chapter 7

1 The relevant texts are available on my website www.holydust.org.

Chapter 8

1 For a discussion of the relation between theology and church architecture, the lavishly illustrated works of Richard Giles are invaluable. Cf. his 1999 and 2004, in Further Reading.

Chapter 9

1 For more on transubstantiation, cf. Herbert McCabe, 'Transubstantiation and Real Presence', in his 1987, *God Matters*, London: Chapman, and the other essays in part 4 of that collection.

2 This obsession is very clear if one compares the drafts for the Church of England's *Common Worship* with the final version, notably in what were once called the 'Offertory Prayers' and in Eucharistic Prayer B.

3 Of course 'reason to believe' means for the Reformers 'recorded in scripture', whereas Catholics allow reason and tradition also to play their part in discerning divine institution; hence the different number of sacraments.

Chapter 10

1 Anonymous medieval rhyme.

2 George Herbert (1593–1633).

3 St Thomas Aquinas, trans. James Woodford (1820–85).

4 Charles Wesley (1707–88).

5 Kevin Nicholls (b. 1929). Reproduced by permission of Kevin Mayhew Ltd, Stowmarket, England.

6 Fred Pratt Green (b. 1903). Reproduced by permission of Stainer and Bell Ltd, London, England.

7 From 'Enemy of Apathy' (Wild Goose Publications, 1988). Words: John L. Bell and Graham Maule © 1988, Wild Goose Resource Group, Iona Community, Glasgow G2 3DH, Scotland. Reproduced by permission.

8 My own poem, from Reflection 4.4, *Last Supper*, in *Skandala: Reflections on Christ*, as yet unpublished. This and other parts of Skandala are available on my website, www.holydust.org.

Chapter 11

1 Cf. modern sociology according to John Milbank, as well as the Darwinian perspectives that regard nature as 'red in tooth and claw', through to Dawkins' notion of 'the selfish gene'.

2 The Church of England report, *Rethinking Sentencing: A contribution to the debate*, 2004, urges a more restorative and less penal approach to criminal justice, though it does not relate the issue to the church's own penitential disciplines.

3 Linda Smith (2003) argues strongly for the place of such oils in the Judeo-Christian tradition.
4 This evocative term derives from Hannah Arendt, who contrasts it with our pre-occupation with 'mortality'.

Chapter 12

1 The notion of the family as 'domestic church' is affirmed by Vatican II, and recent icons of Joseph, Mary and Jesus suggest a human image of the Trinity.
2 The concept derives from Gregory of Nyssa.

Conclusion

1 *The Pierced King*, Meditation 5.2 in my *Skandala*.

Index of Subjects and Names

Index of Biblical References